Purple Church, Red State

Purple Church, Red State

Finding Common Ground in an Age of Polarization

GREG ALLEN-PICKETT

WIPF & STOCK • Eugene, Oregon

PURPLE CHURCH, RED STATE
Finding Common Ground in an Age of Polarization

Wipf & Stock
An Imprint of Wipf and Stock Publishers
199 W. 8th Ave., Suite 3
Eugene, OR 97401

www.wipfandstock.com

PAPERBACK ISBN: 979-8-3852-5687-7
HARDCOVER ISBN: 979-8-3852-5688-4
EBOOK ISBN: 979-8-3852-5689-1

VERSION NUMBER 031326

To the saints of First Presbyterian Church of Hastings,
who have taught me how to lead and love a purple church.

To my wife, Jessica, and my daughter, Esther,
for their steadfast love, patience, and support.

And above all, to God,
from whom all blessings flow.

Contents

Acknowledgements

This book was not written in isolation. It is the fruit of countless conversations, encouragements, and acts of love that have shaped me as a pastor, writer, and disciple of Christ.

I am grateful to my parents, Dean and Cindy Pickett, who instilled in me the conviction that every person bears the inherent value and worth bestowed by our Creator, no matter our differences. That conviction is the heart of this book.

I give thanks for my high school speech and debate coach, Sue Norris, who first taught me how to express myself clearly, carefully, and compassionately. Her lessons echo in every sermon, every pastoral conversation, and every page of this book.

To the Session of First Presbyterian Church of Hastings, particularly those who served in 2020 and 2021 as we navigated the uncertainties of COVID-19 and the conflicts that arose from it: your faith, courage, and perseverance in the midst of challenge taught me what it means to be the church in hard times.

I am indebted to my conversation partners and early readers, including Dr. Dan Deffenbaugh and Kili Wenburg, whose thoughtful feedback sharpened my thinking and strengthened these chapters.

I am thankful for my publisher, Wipf and Stock, and the staff, for their commitment to bringing this book into the world with care.

And finally, to the saints of First Presbyterian Church of Hastings, who welcomed me as your pastor and walked with me through seasons of joy and struggle: this book is as much yours as it is mine.

Introduction

If it is possible, so far as it depends on you, live peaceably with all.
– *Rom 12:18 (NRSV)*

In 2016, Americans awoke to the reality that the ideological divisions in our country had deepened in ways few of us could have imagined. Across kitchen tables, workplaces, and even churches, the polarization that once seemed manageable now felt overwhelming. Families became estranged, friendships unraveled, and the shared bonds that held our communities together grew strained. As the rhetoric intensified, it became easier to retreat into our respective corners—red or blue, conservative or liberal—viewing those on the other side not as neighbors to be loved but as adversaries to be feared or even hated.

It was in this fraught context that I found myself standing at a crossroads, both personally and professionally. In November 2016, I was called to interview for the position of senior pastor at First Presbyterian Church in Hastings, Nebraska. Nestled in the heart of a deep red state, this congregation, like many across the country, was not immune to the pressures of the political and cultural divides that surrounded them. Yet something about their invitation intrigued me. I was captivated by the possibility of serving a church that was not strictly red or blue but, like a delicate brushstroke across a canvas, purple: a blend of passionate convictions, held together by a shared faith and a commitment to community. In this case, the color purple not only represented the blending of the reds and blues of the electoral map; it is also a color that we use in the church during the seasons of Advent and Lent, when we are invited to focus on the birth, life, ministry, death, and resurrection of Christ. This church was choosing to resist the pull of polarization and concentrate on our shared faith and our shared call to be the hands and feet of Jesus in a divided world.

The road that has unfolded over the next eight years was neither smooth nor predictable. From fiery political debates to moments of profound reconciliation, our congregation became a microcosm of the broader challenges and opportunities that face our nation. Together, we wrestled with complex and contentious issues: immigration, gun violence, racism, the role of faith in public life, and many others. And yet, in the midst of these struggles, something remarkable began to take shape: this church in Central Nebraska found its identity and focus on serving Christ by engaging with one another in love and reaching out to its community.

This book is the story of that journey. It is not a tale of easy victories or neat resolutions. Rather, it is an honest account of what it means to seek and find common ground in an age of polarization. It is about the messy, beautiful, frustrating, and grace-filled work of building a "beloved community" in a world that often feels hopelessly divided.

In these pages, you will meet members of our congregation: faithful, flawed, and courageous, who have chosen to lean into the hard work of reconciliation. You will hear stories of neighbors learning to speak each other's languages, both literally and figuratively, and of unlikely partnerships forged in the name of love and justice. You will encounter moments of deep disagreement but also profound grace, as we strive to live out the call to love God and neighbor in tangible, transformative ways.

This book is not just about our church; it is about all of us. It is a call to imagine what might be possible if we dared to listen, to learn, and to love across the divides that separate us. It is a reminder that, even in the most polarized times, there is hope.

Whether you come to this book from a red state, a blue state, or somewhere in between, my prayer is that you will find inspiration, challenge, and encouragement in these pages. May it spark your imagination for what a purple church, or even a purple community, might look like. And may it remind us all that the work of healing and finding common ground is not just necessary; it is holy.

Let us begin.

CHAPTER 1

The Call and the Context

"For God so loved the world that he gave his only Son, so that everyone who believes in him may not perish but may have eternal life. Indeed, God did not send the Son into the world to condemn the world, but in order that the world might be saved through him."

—JOHN 3:16–17 (NRSV)

IN NOVEMBER 2016, AS the dust settled from one of the most polarizing elections in American history, I found myself on a plane to Nebraska. A puddle-jumper descended toward the Central Nebraska Regional Airport, my window offering a view of wide-open skies and patchwork fields. I'd booked the ticket with only the vaguest idea of where I was going, having never set foot in the Cornhusker State. "Grand Island" was a name that hadn't entered my lexicon until it appeared in my travel itinerary. Why was there a town called Grand Island on the Great Plains in a doubly landlocked state so far from the coasts? I had so many questions.

When I stepped off the plane, I was warmly greeted by members of the pastoral search committee from First Presbyterian Church of Hastings. They had come to drive me forty-five minutes through cornfields to their city of 25,000, where I would interview for the role of senior pastor. I was new to Nebraska, new to this cultural landscape, and stepping into what would be my first time serving as the senior pastor of a congregation.

The church had experienced a difficult transition between pastors that reflected the divided cultural and political landscape. They invited a pastoral candidate to a final interview in April of 2016, and the congregation was split on whether to hire that pastor. This split vote reflected a divided and beleaguered congregation. Following the vote and the failed search, attendance began to decline, and church members who had been friends for decades found themselves torn.

Meanwhile, the national landscape was equally unfamiliar, unsettled, and uneasy. The presidential election had thrust the country into a red-and-blue tug-of-war. Nebraska, with its deep crimson shade, voted decisively for Donald Trump, reflecting the broader dynamics of the Great Plains. I'd been told, however, that historically First Presbyterian Church was a tapestry of diverse theological and political perspectives—a kind of microcosm of the nation, where red and blue mingled to form a curious shade of purple.

The weekend of my visit passed in a blur of handshakes, interviews, and questions that hinted at the unspoken challenge: could I shepherd a congregation that didn't always agree with itself, in a state where my presence as an outsider might be met with skepticism? The congregation voted to hire me as their pastor. I accepted, and in March 2017, our family packed up and moved to Hastings.

On March 12, 2017, I stood in the pulpit of First Presbyterian Church of Hastings for the first time as its senior pastor. The sanctuary, a stately yet inviting space with stained glass windows, beautiful organ pipes, and lots of polished dark wood, felt both foreign and familiar as I gazed out at the congregation. I had prepared for weeks, crafting a sermon that I hoped would strike the right balance: faithful yet not too provocative, authentic yet cautious. I opened my sermon saying:

> Good morning, First Presbyterian Church of Hastings. I cannot describe in words the joy and excitement I am feeling this morning as I begin my time as your pastor. I am so grateful for this community, for our shared discernment process that led me and my family here, and for the opportunity you have given me to be your pastor. I hope we will have many years of exploring and growing in our faith together, learning what it means to be a follower of Jesus Christ, making beautiful music together to worship God, and sharing our lives together in this community of faith.
>
> Let's begin that journey this morning. This is the second Sunday in the season of Lent, the forty days leading up to Easter

> when the Christian community focuses on preparing our hearts and minds to reflect on Christ's journey to the cross. It is a time when many Christians prepare for Easter by observing a period of fasting, repentance, moderation, and spiritual discipline. Lent is generally a more somber period in the Christian calendar, and Christ followers are invited to use this time to reflect on our sinfulness before God, our human mortality, and our need for Jesus.
>
> It is against that backdrop that I am preaching my very first sermon as your pastor. In the midst of all the joy and excitement of my first Sunday here, I am being invited by our liturgical calendar to be reminded of my need for Jesus and to invite each of you to do the same. My hope for this season of Lent and my ministry here is that we can focus on our identity as Christians as we prepare for our annual retelling of the passion and Easter story.

One of the assigned texts for the morning included John 3:16–17: "For God so loved the world that he gave his only Son, so that everyone who believes in him may not perish but may have eternal life. Indeed, God did not send the Son into the world to condemn the world, but in order that the world might be saved through him."

I concluded the sermon saying:

> Jesus is describing to all of us what it means to find our central identity as followers of God. To be a follower of God means to be loved. To be a follower of God means to be loved so much that God would work for each of us to not perish but have eternal life. To be a follower of God means that we are not condemned but that we are saved.
>
> So, our central identity as Christians is to be blessed, to be loved, and to be saved. We are blessed when we hear God's call on our lives and respond. The blessing we receive is a blessing of love, a love so deep that it is self-sacrificial. And through that love we are saved. And our response to all of that? I believe we are called to respond in gratitude to these blessings, this love, and our salvation. We are called to in turn be a blessing to others.

It was a "honeymoon" season for all of us: a time to learn each other's rhythms, to test the waters, to build trust. It was also the season of Lent, the six weeks leading up to Easter when we focus on Jesus' life and ministry and his journey to Jerusalem that will lead to his trial, death, crucifixion, and resurrection. The liturgical color for the season of Lent is purple, and I was finding myself living into this purple reality of a politically and theologically diverse "purple" church that reflected not only the electoral map but also the purple of Lent that focused us on the life and ministry of Jesus Christ.

It was the beginning of a journey in a time of reckoning. The polarization that had simmered during the election in 2016 had boiled over at the beginning of a new divisive presidential administration, with debates about crowd sizes at inaugurations and Women's Marches. The world felt different, divided into stark opposites: us versus them, red versus blue, rural versus urban. The divisions ran so deep they could feel insurmountable.

I soon realized that my calling in Hastings would not be merely to preach the gospel but to learn from my church members how to *embody* it in a way that bridges divides. Over the last eight years, our church's ministry and witness has become an experiment in cultivating reconciliation in a fractured world. The results have often been humbling, sometimes rewarding, and occasionally messy. But the congregation of First Presbyterian Church has taught me, our members, and our community something vital: that the church can still be a place where different voices come together, not to argue but to listen; not to win but to heal.

I like to think of First Presbyterian Church of Hastings as a canvas, one where we dare to paint a different picture than the one the world seems to demand. In a time of entrenched lines of division, we try to color outside the lines, finding unity in unexpected places and sowing seeds of hope in the rich soil of the Nebraska plains, grounded in our call to serve. The canvas of our church, our community, and our country is still a work in progress. Hopefully we can continue to paint a masterpiece that reflects the beauty of our diversity while also breaking free of the lines that divide us to blend our shared hopes and dreams together.

Discussion Questions:

1. Reflecting on the divisions in our nation during 2016 and beyond, what are some ways faith communities can serve as spaces for reconciliation and healing? Where have you seen this done well, and where is there room for growth?
2. The chapter describes the congregation as a "curious shade of purple," where red and blue perspectives mingle. How does your faith shape the way you engage with those who hold different perspectives, especially in times of tension?

3. What challenges and opportunities arise when trying to find unity in diversity, whether in a church, community, or family? How do you balance authenticity in your own convictions with openness to others?
4. The chapter recalls the "honeymoon season" of a new pastorate, filled with hope, trust-building, and fresh energy. How can seasons of new beginnings, whether in leadership, relationships, or communities, be used to lay a foundation for deeper reconciliation and growth?
5. The image of the church as a canvas—painting outside the lines, blending colors, creating something new—suggests a different way of seeing community. How might this metaphor inspire us to imagine our own congregation or community differently? What picture are we painting together, and how does it reflect (or fail to reflect) God's love?

Reflection on John 3:16–17 and Chapter 1

John 3:16 is perhaps the most familiar verse in all of Scripture. We see it on signs at sporting events, etched into church walls, and even on bumper stickers. Its familiarity can sometimes make us miss its radical depth. "For God so loved the world that he gave his only Son, so that everyone who believes in him may not perish but may have eternal life."

But the next verse is equally important: "Indeed, God did not send the Son into the world to condemn the world, but in order that the world might be saved through him." Together, these verses remind us of God's central posture toward creation: not condemnation but love. Not rejection but redemption.

When I stood in the pulpit for the first time as pastor of First Presbyterian Church of Hastings in March 2017, this was the text the lectionary gave me. In a moment when our nation was deeply divided, when my new congregation was still healing from its own internal divisions, and when my own heart was full of both nervousness and hope, I could not have asked for a better passage. The gospel gave me words to say: our identity as Christians is not grounded in our political affiliation, our theological position, or our social background. Our identity is this: we are loved. We are loved so much that God gave his Son. We are loved not for our perfection but in spite of our imperfection. We are loved not to be condemned but to be saved.

In those early days, it felt like a honeymoon season. We were learning one another's rhythms, finding joy in worship, and discovering what ministry together might look like. But beneath the surface, the reality of polarization was real, both nationally and locally. The temptation was to let those divisions define us. But John's Gospel insists on a different starting point. Before we are red or blue, conservative or progressive, urban or rural, we are beloved children of God.

This is why John 3:16–17 is more than a slogan. It is a foundation. If God's posture toward the world is love, then our posture toward one another must also be love. If God sent Jesus not to condemn but to save, then the church must also resist the temptation to condemn and instead seek to reconcile, to heal, to bless.

That has become the calling of our congregation in Hastings: to be a purple church in a red state, to paint a different picture than the world demands, to model what it means to live as loved people who love in return. Our ministry has not been perfect. It has often been messy. But in the end, the gospel is clear. Our central identity is not our division but our salvation. Not condemnation but grace. Not fear but love.

"For God so loved the world." Not some of the world. Not the part of the world that thinks like us. The whole world. All of us. That love is the masterpiece God is still painting, and we are called to join in, blending our colors together in the bond of Christ's redeeming love.

Chapter 2

Peanut Butter and Jelly

Uniting a Church in Service

I beg you to lead a life worthy of the calling to which you have been called, with all humility and gentleness, with patience, bearing with one another in love, making every effort to maintain the unity of the Spirit in the bond of peace. There is one body and one Spirit, just as you were called to the one hope of your calling.

—*Eph 4:1–4 (NRSV)*

The first five months in Hastings really did feel like a honeymoon. I was adjusting to the congregation as the congregation was adjusting to me. In May, the mission committee started talking about getting ready for "Open Table" sack lunch packing this summer. I remembered stories of this beautiful ministry from my interviews.

Every Sunday in July, after the final hymn and benediction, a joyful transformation takes place at First Presbyterian Church of Hastings. The sanctuary, still resonant with the morning's worship, empties as people head to the fellowship hall. There, tables are arranged with assembly-line precision, laden with jars of peanut butter and jelly, stacks of bread, baggies, bags of chips, cups of pudding, and brown paper sacks. It is time to pack sack lunches for the Open Table program.

On these Sundays, the church hums with activity. Children dart between tables, eager to help, while adults settle into their stations, spreading peanut butter and jelly, stuffing bags, and sealing lunch sacks. It is a scene of organized chaos, fueled by laughter, chatter, and the occasional song. By the end of each Sunday in July, over 1,200 lunches are packed, and by month's end, the total exceeds 5,000. These lunches go to Catholic Social Services, where they are distributed to anyone in need, especially children who rely on free school lunches during the academic year and face hunger during the summer months.

But these Sundays are about more than sandwiches. They are about community. Over the years, the Open Table sack lunch program has become a microcosm of what makes this church remarkable: people of starkly different political and theological beliefs sitting side by side, united by a shared mission to feed hungry people in our community. In a congregation that had struggled with division, this simple act of service became a lifeline, a tangible expression of the unity Paul speaks of in his letter to the Ephesians: "I beg you to lead a life worthy of the calling to which you have been called, with all humility and gentleness, with patience, bearing with one another in love, making every effort to maintain the unity of the Spirit in the bond of peace."

The Open Table program itself was not started by First Presbyterian Church. It began as a community initiative nearly two decades ago, when leaders and volunteers from Catholic Social Services, the Crossroads homeless shelter, Saint Mark's Episcopal Church, and other community organizations and leaders came together to address the hunger facing the residents of Hastings. Their collaboration gave birth to what has become one of the most enduring and unifying ministries in our town.

About fifteen years ago, someone at First Presbyterian spoke up and said, "We could help with this." Our church joined the coalition, committing to take one month each year to provide thousands of sack lunches. That decision connected our congregation to a larger effort that was already feeding families across Hastings.

One Sunday, I watched as two men, let us call them Jim and Will, worked side by side. Jim, a staunch conservative, wore his politics on his sleeve, often voicing his concerns about government overreach. Will, a progressive retired teacher, had marched in protests and advocated for increased social programs. In another context, their interactions might have been tense. But here, their differences melted away. Jim's booming laugh echoed through the hall as he handed Will a jar of peanut butter. "Think we will pack 1,500 sack lunches today?" he asked. Will grinned. "Not if you keep talking instead of spreading."

Then there are Mary and Linda, whose theological perspectives are as different as night and day. Mary's faith is rooted in tradition, a more literal interpretation of the Bible, and she prefers traditional hymns sung from the pews. Linda embraces contemporary worship and challenges interpretations of Scripture. Yet, as they packed sandwiches, they exchanged stories about their grandchildren, offering each other advice and laughter.

The Open Table program serves as a poignant reminder that our shared humanity can transcend the barriers that divide us. It is hard to argue about politics or theology when your hands are sticky with peanut butter and your focus is on ensuring each sack holds not just food but also hope.

Statistics remind us why this work matters. In Hastings Public Schools, over 60 percent of students qualify for the federal free and reduced lunch program. During the school year, these kids can rely on at least one or two good meals a day served at the school, but in the summer, some of them go hungry. This reality, higher than the state and national averages, weighs heavily on our congregation's heart.

On the first Sunday in July 2017, at the suggestion of a congregation member, I preached a sermon that used Barry Manilow's song "One Voice," pairing it with Rom 15 and Eph 4, reflecting Paul's call to unity. The lyrics speak of a single voice starting a song, joined by others until it becomes a chorus. For our congregation, that one voice was the person on the mission committee suggesting that our church join the Open Table coalition. We were not the first voice, but by adding ours, the chorus grew stronger. That single decision has become a sustained commitment, a chorus of service, and a witness of God's love.

In Rom 15, Paul offers a vision of this unity: "Each of us must please our neighbor for the good purpose of building up the neighbor … May the God of steadfastness and encouragement grant you to live in harmony with one another, in accordance with Christ Jesus, so that together you may with one voice glorify the God and Father of our Lord Jesus Christ."

This harmony is not easy. It requires humility, gentleness, and patience. It demands that we bear with one another in love, even when it is hard. But as I have witnessed time and again at the Open Table, it is possible. And it is beautiful.

Part of what makes ministries like Open Table so powerful is that they invite us to live our faith with our hands as much as with our heads. Packing sack lunches may seem like an ordinary task, but in those moments of service the body of Christ becomes visible. When our hands are busy serving, our hearts often open in ways that would be harder in a heated debate or a difficult conversation. Doing the work of Christ together by spreading peanut butter, bagging chips, or tying off a sack lunch creates a natural space for unity. We discover that it is difficult to demonize someone across the political aisle when you are working shoulder to shoulder with them to feed a hungry child.

That kind of embodied discipleship matters in an age of polarization. So much of our world encourages us to sort ourselves by categories, opinions, or votes. The church is called to offer a different way. When we show up to serve together, the focus shifts away from what divides us and toward the common mission of following Christ. We find ourselves less concerned with winning an argument and more committed to making sure a hungry person has something to eat.

This is what it means to be the church: not a group of people who all think alike but a community of disciples willing to put their hands, hearts, and lives into the service of God and neighbor.

As our church continues to wrestle with its differences, our participation in the Open Table program serves as a beacon of hope. It reminds us that we are called to something greater than ourselves. Together, we can live in harmony, not by ignoring our differences but by focusing on our shared mission: to love God and neighbor.

Discussion Questions:

1. How does the act of serving others, such as packing lunches for the Open Table program, help bridge differences among people with opposing political or theological views? Can you think of other examples where shared service has fostered unity in your own life or community?
2. The Open Table program began as a community-wide initiative. What does this reveal about the power of collaboration across congregations and organizations?

3. The chapter describes moments of connection, like Jim and Will laughing together or Mary and Linda exchanging stories. What do these interactions teach us about focusing on our shared humanity rather than our differences?
4. Paul's message in Eph 4 and Rom 15 calls for unity, humility, and love. How do these passages resonate with the story of the Open Table program? In what ways does this ministry reflect the principles of Christian community?
5. The chapter discusses the statistics about hunger in Hastings and the congregation's response to this need. What does this reveal about the role of the church in addressing systemic issues like food insecurity? How can your own faith community or an organization you are a part of take similar actions to meet the needs of your neighbors?

Reflection on Eph 4:1–4 and Chapter 2

In his letter to the Ephesians, Paul pleads with the church: "Lead a life worthy of the calling to which you have been called, with all humility and gentleness, with patience, bearing with one another in love, making every effort to maintain the unity of the Spirit in the bond of peace. There is one body and one Spirit, just as you were called to the one hope of your calling."

These words are not abstract theology. They are instructions for how to live faithfully together as Christ's body, especially when differences threaten to divide us. Unity, Paul insists, does not mean uniformity. It is not about erasing distinctions but about weaving them together into a common life animated by humility, patience, and love.

I have seen this unity embodied in the Open Table sack lunch program. Each July, our sanctuary empties into the fellowship hall and becomes a bustling workshop of discipleship. Children spread peanut butter, adults bag chips, grandparents seal lunch sacks. Side by side, people who disagree about politics or theology serve together with sticky hands and open hearts. Over the course of the month, more than 5,000 lunches are prepared, destined for children who might otherwise go hungry during the summer.

In those moments, Paul's vision comes to life. Jim, the outspoken conservative, and Will, the progressive retired teacher, laugh together as they pass jars of peanut butter. Mary, who clings to the traditions of the faith, and Linda, who embraces new expressions, swap stories about their grandchildren as they pack lunches. Their unity does not erase their differences, but their service reframes them. The Spirit binds them together, not in argument but in shared mission.

This is what it means to live a life worthy of our calling. Not to win debates but to build bridges. Not to seek our own way but to bear with one another in love. Not to divide along the world's fault lines but to discover the deeper bond that comes from serving Christ together.

At Open Table, sack lunches become sacraments: ordinary elements transformed by extraordinary grace. Each sandwich is an offering, each bag of chips a prayer, each brown sack a small proclamation of the gospel: that there is one body, one Spirit, and one hope that calls us into unity.

In a polarized age, the church's witness is not only in what we say but in what we do together. When we lead with humility, when we practice patience, when we bear with one another in love, we become living proof of Paul's words. We show the world that Christ's body is one and that one Spirit still binds us in peace.

Chapter 3

Confronting Racism

Charlottesville and Flyers in Hastings

So God created humankind in his image, in the image of God he created them; male and female he created them.

—*Gen 1:27 (NRSV)*

See what love the Father has given us, that we should be called children of God; and that is what we are.

—*1 John 3:1 (NRSV)*

For the first five months, I kept my preaching relatively centrist, avoiding overt references to the polarizing political climate. Instead, I participated in unifying events like the Open Table sack lunch program and leaned into the rich resources of our tradition: hymns, prayers, and liturgy that spoke to justice, mercy, and humility without explicitly naming the fractures in our national life. I also sought to ground all of my preaching in Scripture, which provides plenty of food for thought and is equally appreciated by conservatives and liberals. My hope was that these elements would plant seeds of reflection and dialogue.

But then came August 2017. Whatever sense of equilibrium we had achieved was shattered by the events of that month, beginning with the white supremacist marches in Charlottesville, Virginia.

The footage began to circulate late Friday evening, August 11. Torchlight processions of mostly young white men snaked through the University of Virginia's campus, chanting slogans that sent chills down our collective spine as a nation: "Jews will not replace us," "You will not replace us," and "Blood and soil." The next day, chaos erupted as counter-protesters clashed with marchers carrying Confederate flags and swastikas. By Saturday afternoon, the violence turned deadly when a car intentionally rammed into a crowd of peaceful counter-protesters, killing 32-year-old Heather Heyer and injuring dozens more.

By Sunday morning, I knew that what had unfolded in Charlottesville was a moment of reckoning for our country. But I also knew that my congregation, like the rest of the nation, was still processing the events. The details were murky, the emotions raw. I decided not to address Charlottesville directly in my sermon that day. Instead, I stayed with the lectionary text and offered prayers for peace, justice, and reconciliation. It felt inadequate, but at the time, it seemed prudent to wait.

That prudence lasted only a few hours. By Sunday afternoon, the national conversation shifted dramatically, and I realized that silence was no longer an option. The question was no longer whether to respond but how.

The answer came just a few days later. Early Wednesday morning, the people of Hastings woke to find racist flyers posted around town. They were taped to lampposts near the high school. The flyers, crudely printed and hateful in tone, warned of the supposed dangers posed by immigrants and minorities. They featured white nationalist slogans and urged readers to "defend their heritage."

While the flyers were abhorrent, they localized the issue in a way that made it impossible to ignore. This wasn't just about Charlottesville; racism was in our own backyard. The flyers became a turning point for me, for our church, and for our community.

I sat down and drafted a statement opposing racism and white supremacy:

> As faith leaders in the Hastings community, we believe that God is sovereign over all creation, and because all human beings are embraced by God's all-encompassing grace, anything reflecting white nationalism, white supremacy, or hate and discrimination

towards another human being does not reflect the God revealed in our Scriptures.

Regardless of our specific political persuasions, we agree that the attitudes fostered by any manifestation of white nationalism are inconsistent with Christian values of welcoming the stranger as if we were welcoming Christ. That commitment stems from our biblical faith. In Matt 25, Jesus called upon his followers to feed the hungry, give drink to the thirsty, and show hospitality to the stranger. He reminded his disciples that whenever they do any of these things "to the least of these, my brothers and sisters," they are doing them for Christ himself.

In the apostle Paul's letter to the Galatians (3:28), he reminds us that there is no differentiation between any ethnic group or social class—Jews and Gentiles, slaves and free, male or female—because we are all one in Christ Jesus.

We believe that every human being is a precious child of God (1 John 3:1), made in the image of God (Gen 1:27). God believes that every human being is deserving of God's love, and God calls on each of us to practice the same. We are called to see the image of God in every person we meet, and that should compel us to treat every person with dignity and respect and to reach out in love, remembering that we love because God first loved us (1 John 4:19)

In the values purported by these groups, we see no public witness consistent with the Gospel or with the values of those who are believers in Jesus Christ and members of Christ's church. As faith leaders in the community of Hastings, we stand firmly against any articulation or manifestation of white supremacy, white nationalism, or hate groups in our community.

We also renew our commitment to a future where faith communities and faith leaders will foster attitudes and actions so that all human beings and the whole of creation can thrive. We join our prayers, our hearts, our minds, our voices, and our actions with other people of faith, as well as with secular people of good conscience, to resist the present destructive forces in our country manifest in these messages and images from groups representing white supremacy and hate in our country.

Through the power of God's infinite love and the invitation that God gives us to do justice, embrace compassion, and walk humbly with God (Mic 6:8), we seek to be a force for positive good in our community and to reverse the destructive consequences of these groups here in our community, in our state and country, and around the world.

I shared this statement with the leadership council of my church, and they endorsed it, as well as my plan to invite other faith leaders to sign it.

I started reaching out in the community, trying to connect with other pastors. The city of Hastings doesn't have a formal "ministerial alliance," in part because of the polarization that reached into our churches. Some of the more conservative evangelical churches didn't see value in collaborating with the centrist mainline churches, and a lot of pastors were so busy leading their churches, they didn't have time to come together. So I scoured local church websites for the email addresses of other pastors and sent an invitation to thirty-two pastors in Hastings to sign on to this statement, publish it in the newspaper, and join me for a press conference where we would read the statement aloud on the steps of City Hall. My hope was that a group of faith leaders standing in unity, opposing racism would send a clear message and that anyone who agreed with the sentiment on the flyers would see their pastors standing up and publicly denouncing that perspective, which would hopefully lead to repentance.

One pastor in town picked up the phone and asked me what I was doing and why I was doing this. He came from a more progressive faith tradition and expressed that he was concerned for my ministry and leadership. He felt I shouldn't be attempting to make such a bold proclamation this early in my tenure at the church and in the community.

One pastor from a more conservative faith tradition replied directly to me and wrote:

> If the fliers were posted by someone from this community (which I doubt), the views reflected by those statements are the views of a tiny, tiny, tiny segment of the local population. If someone had simply removed the fliers and deposited them in the garbage where they belong, life in Hastings could continue as normal. Instead, the entire state is now up in arms that Hastings has been infiltrated by white supremacist hatemongers, all because a deranged idiot posted a couple of fliers. Thanks to you, that deranged idiot has gotten more publicity than he could have hoped for. Sorry Greg, you do not have my support for your statement.

Another pastor "replied all" to the group email and wrote:

> I write in response to your efforts to mobilize Hastings clergy to make a public statement against the white supremacist signs posted around town recently. I abhor using Christ to justify racism, but I did not join in the protest; allow me to explain why:

1. Barna-group studies like UnChristian and You Lost Me identify the politicization of American Evangelicalism as the primary reason why increasing percentages of Millennials, whether raised in church or not, are rejecting church-going. The most memorable quote from one of the books: "If Christianity is all about conservative politics, I'm outta here." Resisting white supremacy is less open to the charge of pushing a Moral-Majority-style social and political agenda, but I am leery of publicly politicizing my ministry and message.
2. I mean this humbly rather than judgmentally, but frankly, I am also leery of making common cause with ministers who advocate social, political, moral, or theological agenda that I cannot endorse.

It became clear to me that the polarization in our nation had also reached deeply into the local churches in my newly adopted community.

However, in addition to these negative responses, I also received positive responses from twenty pastors from various denominations across the theological and political spectrum. They agreed to sign on to the statement, which was submitted to the newspaper and published on Friday, August 18. We called a press conference, gathered on the steps of city hall, read the statement, and took questions from the press.

In addition to faith leaders and members of the media that attended, a dozen members of my church showed up, including members of the mission committee and the leadership council. This helped me to know that I was on the right track and that our church was sincerely interested in engaging our minds and our hearts around these contentious issues.

That week, I also crafted a sermon that I knew would be risky. I wrestled with the biblical text, prayed fervently, and sought wisdom from colleagues and mentors. The words came slowly at first, but eventually, the sermon began to take shape. I decided to root my message in the parable of the good Samaritan, a story that calls us to expand our definition of neighbor and to confront the boundaries we draw around our compassion.

On Sunday, August 20, I stepped into the pulpit with a mix of resolve and trepidation. I began by naming the events of the past week: the marches in Charlottesville and the flyers in Hastings. I did not mince words, and I called racism what it is: a sin. I acknowledged the fear and anger that many were feeling, but I also challenged the congregation to look inward, to examine the ways in which prejudice and indifference can take root in our own hearts.

I quoted Rev. Dr. Martin Luther King Jr., who said, "Injustice anywhere is a threat to justice everywhere." I reminded the congregation that as followers of Christ, we are called to speak out against injustice, even when it is uncomfortable or unpopular. I spoke of the good Samaritan, who did not walk away from the wounded man on the roadside but instead crossed boundaries of ethnicity and enmity to offer care. "The question," I said, "is not, 'Who is my neighbor?' but rather, 'How can I be a neighbor?' In a time when hatred and division seek to define us, we are called to embody a different story, a story of love, courage, and justice."

The response was varied. Some members of the congregation thanked me for addressing the issue head-on. Others expressed discomfort, questioning whether it was appropriate to "bring politics into the pulpit." One longtime member pulled me aside after the service and said, "I've been coming to this church for forty years, and I've never heard a sermon like that. It made me think. Thank you."

Not everyone was so affirming. A few members sent emails expressing their displeasure at the statement and press conference earlier in the week, accusing me of being too political. One person stopped attending altogether. These reactions stung, but they also underscored the importance of what we were trying to do. If the gospel does not challenge us, if it does not push us out of our comfort zones, then are we truly living it?

The events of that week set the tone for the years to come. They marked the beginning of our church's journey to confront the systemic injustices in our community and beyond. In the months that followed, we began hosting conversations about race, privilege, and reconciliation. We doubled down on our partnerships with local organizations to support immigrant and refugee families and advocate for racial equity. We became more intentional in our worship, incorporating prayers, hymns, and liturgies that reflected our commitment to justice and inclusion.

Looking back, I see that week as a crucible: a moment that tested our courage and clarified our calling. It was not easy, and it was not without cost. But it was necessary. For in the face of hatred, silence is complicity. And in the face of division, the church must be a beacon of unity and hope.

The racist flyers were removed, but their impact lingered. They served as a stark reminder that the work of confronting racism is not a one-time event but a lifelong journey. It is work that requires humility, persistence, and a willingness to listen and learn. It is work that begins in our own hearts and extends to the broader community.

In the years since that first test, our church has often returned to the story of the good Samaritan. We have thought about the courage it takes to stop on the roadside, to see the humanity in someone who is different, and to extend compassion in the face of danger. That is the work we are called to as the church. It is not always comfortable and it is rarely easy, but it is the work of the gospel. And it is the work that can transform a fractured world into a beloved community. In Hastings, Nebraska, on that week in August, we took our first steps on that journey. And while the road ahead would be long and winding, we walk it together, trusting that the Spirit is guiding us, challenging us, and sustaining us along the way.

Discussion Questions:

1. Have you or has your church ever been in a situation where you had to take a public stand on an issue that might have been divisive? How did you navigate the risks and rewards?
2. What do you think about the concerns raised by the pastors who chose not to sign the statement? Are their hesitations valid, or do you disagree with their stance?
3. How does the parable of the good Samaritan challenge us to rethink our definition of "neighbor" in today's context?
4. There were a variety of reactions from the congregation—support, discomfort, and even resistance. How can church leaders foster constructive dialogue in polarized settings?
5. How do you interpret the tension between keeping religion "apolitical" and addressing deeply moral issues like racism and hatred?

Reflection on 1 John 3:1, Gen 1:27, and Chapter 3

In August 2017, when white nationalist flyers appeared on the streets of Hastings, our community was forced to face a painful truth: the poison of racism was not only "out there" in distant cities but right here in our own backyard. In that moment, silence was not an option. As pastors, we came together and declared a truth that is as old as Scripture itself:

> "We believe that every human being is a precious child of God (1 John 3:1), made in the image of God (Gen 1:27). We are called to

> see the image of God in every person we meet, and that should compel us to treat every person with dignity and respect and to reach out in love, remembering that we love because God first loved us." (1 John 4:19).

This conviction runs like a golden thread through the entire Bible. In Gen 1, the creation story climaxes with God's declaration that humanity, male and female, every tribe and tongue, bears the divine image. To see another person is to see a reflection of God. In 1 John 3, we are reminded that this identity is not just abstract theology but a relational reality: "See what love the Father has given us, that we should be called children of God; and that is what we are." Every human being, regardless of race or heritage, is embraced by that love.

The call to live this out in daily life is clear. When Jesus told the parable of the good Samaritan (Luke 10:25–37), he asked his followers to see neighborliness not in terms of shared ethnicity or ideology but in concrete acts of compassion across boundaries. When Paul proclaimed to the Galatians that "there is no longer Jew or Greek, slave or free, male or female, for you are all one in Christ Jesus" (Gal 3:28), he named the radical unity that Christ makes possible. And when Jesus, in Matt 25, identified himself with "the least of these"—the hungry, the thirsty, the stranger, the prisoner—he taught that our love for God is revealed in our love for the most vulnerable.

That is why the statement we made was not political theater but gospel witness. Racism, white nationalism, and xenophobia contradict the very core of Christian faith. To remain silent in the face of such hatred would be to deny what Scripture so clearly teaches: that every person is beloved, every person bears God's image, and every person is worthy of dignity and love.

Of course, speaking these truths has costs. Some in our community thanked us for our courage; others accused us of politicizing the pulpit. Yet Scripture reminds us that love is not passive. Love bears witness. Love crosses lines. Love risks discomfort for the sake of the vulnerable. As Mic 6:8 declares, God has already shown us what is good: "To do justice, to love kindness, and to walk humbly with your God."

Looking back, that August week in Hastings was a crucible for our congregation and for me as a pastor. It was a moment when the gospel's demands became impossible to ignore. And though the work of dismantling racism is long and unfinished, we continue to return to this foundation: every human being is a child of God, made in God's image, loved before we ever loved in return. To live as if that were true is the vocation of the church in every age.

Chapter 4

Crossing Cultures

Spanish Classes, Folkloric Dance, and Tacos

Let mutual love continue. Do not neglect to show hospitality to strangers, for by doing that some have entertained angels without knowing it.

—*Heb 13:1–2 (NRSV)*

When I arrived in Hastings, I felt a tension of disconnection. The town had changed over the years, with 14 percent of the population identifying as Hispanic or Latino according to the latest census and the schools were reporting even higher numbers. Yet, on Sunday mornings, our congregation did not reflect those demographics. This disparity gnawed at me as someone who had lived and worked in Ecuador and Guatemala and had also spent time working with and learning from my Spanish-speaking sisters and brothers in the United States. It seemed we were missing an opportunity to reflect the kingdom of God in all its beautiful diversity. I brought this concern to the mission committee during my first year. "Why don't we see more of our Hispanic neighbors in church?" I asked.

There was a moment of silence. Then, one of our long-serving members spoke up. "Maybe they don't feel welcome," she said. "Not intentionally, of course, but… if I moved to a new country and didn't know the language or the culture, I don't think I'd walk into a strange church either." Her words hung in the air, convicting and energizing us at the same time.

In previous churches, I had seen English as a Second Language (ESL) classes serve as bridges between congregations and immigrant communities. But upon some investigation we realized that Hastings already had several excellent ESL programs. We didn't want to duplicate efforts unnecessarily. "What if we flipped it?" someone suggested. "Instead of offering ESL classes, what if we teach Spanish to our members?" The idea resonated. By learning Spanish, we could extend a hand of friendship in the language of our neighbors. It was a way of saying, "We see you, and we're willing to meet you where you are."

About the same time, one of our sassy, social-justice-loving octogenarians, Jane, attended a rally welcoming immigrants. Jane, with her trademark spark and curiosity, struck up a conversation with a woman named Berta, a Mexican-American immigrant. When Jane shared our budding idea of Spanish classes, Berta's face lit up. "I'd love to help," Berta said. "I could teach the classes for free. This is something I believe in."

Two weeks later, Berta stood at the front of our fellowship hall, introducing herself to a group of six eager learners. She began with simple greetings: "Hola, ¿cómo están?" "What's that mean?" asked a retired farmer who admitted he'd never spoken a word of Spanish in his life. "It means, 'Hi, how are you?'" Berta explained. He nodded and repeated the phrase carefully, his accent thick but his enthusiasm genuine.

Week by week, our little class grew. It wasn't just about learning a language; it was about building relationships. Soon word got out in the community and it wasn't just members of our church who attended but community members who wanted to learn Spanish so they could talk to their neighbors. This included a nurse working in our hospital and a family that was planning a trip to South America later in the year. Berta brought friends along to serve as tutors. In addition to teaching language, they shared stories of their own journey: the struggles of adapting to a new culture and the joys of raising their families in Hastings. The class members, in turn, shared their stories. It wasn't long before the class felt less like a lesson and more like a gathering of friends.

One evening, as class was wrapping up, Berta's eyes sparkled with an idea. "You know," she said, "There's a Mexican folkloric dance troupe in town. Currently they practice outdoors on the sidewalk in the trailer court, but it is getting cold. They're always looking for places to practice and perform. Would the church be interested in hosting them, providing a place for them to practice? In return, they could dance for your church during a worship service." The mission committee jumped at the idea. Hosting the dance troupe could be another way to build bridges and celebrate the rich cultural heritage of our Hispanic neighbors.

When the Mexican folkloric dance troupe first arrived, our church came alive with color and movement. The dancers wore traditional outfits: women in vibrant, swirling skirts adorned with ribbons and men in sombreros and embroidered shirts. The first practice felt like a cultural awakening for our congregation. They used space in the church's community center to practice for a number of months. A few members of our church joined them and learned to dance, while others came to open up the building for their rehearsals and stayed to interact with the dancers and their families. The space they were using was filled with their joyful dancing, music, and laughter, and they began to feel like First Presbyterian Church was their home.

After six months of rehearsing in the church, they were invited to dance during a Sunday morning worship service. First Presbyterian Church of Hastings is a relatively traditional church with a historic sanctuary, traditional music led by an organ and choir, and worship that is spirit-filled but usually pretty calm. On this morning, the sanctuary filled with the sounds of lively music. The dancers moved with grace and energy, their skirts sweeping the floor in unison. Our congregation, many of whom had never experienced anything like it, responded with applause. Afterward, the dancers and their families stayed for a potluck meal that we had scheduled that morning. At that first potluck, I watched connections form over shared plates of tamales and casseroles.

Over time, these interactions became more frequent and natural. Twice a year, the dance troupe performs in worship, and each time, the potluck that follows is beginning to feel more and more like a family reunion. These interactions put a human face to the headlines about immigrants and brought us closer to our neighbors. Rather than being a polarizing political issue, our politically diverse church was experiencing immigrants through the lens of our shared humanity and living out the call that Jesus puts on us in Matt 25 to welcome the stranger.

A few months after the folkloric dancers had performed in worship for the first time, I received a call at the church office from a familiar voice. It was Beto, a waiter at one of the local Mexican restaurants where my family often dined. We'd shared many friendly conversations over chips and salsa, and now he was calling with an idea. Beto was starting his own business, a taco truck, and he was looking for a place to park it. He'd thought of our church. "Your parking lot is on a busy street," he said, "and people know your church. I think it could work well."

Our parking lot, situated on one of the main thoroughfares in Hastings, is rarely full during the week. The idea made a kind of practical sense. But it was more than practical; it felt like another nudge from the Spirit. I invited Beto to write up a short proposal, which I then brought to the church's leadership council.

At the next council meeting, we had a thoughtful and wide-ranging discussion. Some were concerned about traffic or trash, others about setting precedent. But then someone brought up Heb 13:2: "Do not forget to show hospitality to strangers, for by so doing some have entertained angels without knowing it." That shifted the tone. We began talking less about logistics and more about hospitality, not just to Beto, but to the dozens, perhaps hundreds, of people who might gather on our property to enjoy his tacos. One elder connected it back to the folkloric dance troupe and said, "We opened our building to music and dancing; maybe this is a chance to open our parking lot to the smells and tastes of hospitality."

Another elder added, "What if this is how we continue to build relationships with our neighbors, over carne asada and tortillas?" That brought laughter and a murmur of agreement. In the end, we voted to offer Beto a trial period of six months, with the option to renew if things went well.

They went better than well.

Within weeks of opening, Beto's Tacos became a local favorite. The church parking lot, which had once been a quiet stretch of asphalt during the week, began to buzz with life each lunchtime and evening. Long lines of people—construction workers, hospital staff, families with kids in tow—all waited patiently for their turn to order. The smell of grilled meat and roasted peppers filled the air. Some folks sat in their cars to eat, while others stood around chatting. Beto added some picnic tables underneath a tree in the far corner of the parking lot that got a lot of use. A few of our church members made it a habit to stop by and get lunch once or twice a week: not just for the tacos but for the chance to visit with Beto and his crew.

One afternoon, I walked out to check in on how things were going and found a circle of people, some of whom I knew from church, others I didn't, laughing and swapping stories around the picnic tables under the shade of the old elm tree. A couple of preschoolers were dancing to the upbeat Latin music playing from a speaker in the truck. Someone handed me a taco *al pastor* and said, "You've gotta try this." And in that moment, I realized: this wasn't just a taco truck in a church parking lot. This was fellowship.

Over time, the presence of the taco truck deepened our church's witness. Members who were initially skeptical began to see the value not just economically or culturally but spiritually. Beto became more than a vendor; he became a partner in ministry. He started to recognize people from the dance troupe, from the Spanish classes, from the potlucks.

By the time we reached the end of the six-month trial period, the decision to extend the partnership was unanimous. Beto was part of our story now. And more than that, the community had begun to associate First Presbyterian Church not just with Sunday morning services but with music, dance, language, and now, tacos. The church was becoming, slowly but surely, a place of intersection. A place where people from different backgrounds and cultures crossed paths and shared something meaningful.

As our relationship with the Hispanic community deepened, word spread. One day, we received a call from the local health department. They wanted to host quarterly health seminars in Spanish on topics like diabetes, heart disease, and vaccinations. "We asked the leaders in the Hispanic community where they'd feel most comfortable attending these seminars," the health department representative explained. "They all said First Presbyterian Church." Hearing this brought tears to my eyes. Our church, once disconnected from this vibrant part of our community, had become a place of trust and safety.

One story from these experiences that particularly stands out is that of Jenni, a retired speech language pathologist, and Maria, the leader of the dance troupe. Jenni had taken our Spanish classes and was determined to practice her new language skills, so she volunteered to open the church up for the rehearsals of the Mexican folkloric dance troupe. After a few Spanish classes, she was unlocking the church door to let the dancers into the church, and she introduced herself to Maria in halting Spanish. Maria's face lit up. "¡Muy bien, Jenni!" she said. The two women sat together, with Maria patiently helping Jenni form sentences. Over time, their friendship blossomed. Jenni has attended many of Maria's family gatherings, where she has tried homemade Mexican food for the first time. "I've never tasted anything so good," Jenni later told me, laughing. "And Maria said I'm part of her family now."

These connections formed through our Spanish classes and partnership with the folkloric dance troupe reminded us of the power of simple acts—learning a new language, sharing a meal, or hosting a dance performance—to break down barriers and build bridges.

Paul's words in Rom 12:4–5 are embodied in these moments: "For as in one body we have many members, and not all the members have the same function, so we, who are many, are one body in Christ, and individually we are members one of another."

We still wrestle with our differences, and we have yet to fully incorporate our Hispanic sisters and brothers into the life of our church, but through efforts like these, we're learning what it means to live as one body—diverse yet united in Christ. And every time I see Jenni and Maria laughing together, I am reminded that God's kingdom is richer and more beautiful than we can imagine.

Discussion Questions:

1. What barriers—both visible and invisible—might prevent people from feeling welcome in a community? How can your church or organization take steps to bridge cultural, linguistic, and ideological divides?
2. How did learning Spanish and partnering with the folkloric dance troupe transform relationships between members of the church and the Hispanic community? How did it transform the church? What does this teach us about the power of shared experiences?
3. How can small, personal interactions like the friendship between Jenni and Maria pave the way for larger communal changes?
4. Paul's message in Rom 12:4–5 speaks to the unity of the body of Christ despite differences. How does this Scripture inform the church's approach to diversity, both culturally and ideologically?
5. What role should the church play in building trust and becoming a place of safety for marginalized communities? How can the lessons from this chapter inspire your congregation or organization to fulfill that role more effectively?

Reflection on Heb 13:1–2 and Chapter 4

The writer of Hebrews reminds us that hospitality is not optional for the people of God. It is central to our life of faith. Hospitality is more than politeness or good manners. It is the holy practice of making space: space in our homes, space in our churches, and space in our lives for those who are new, different, or overlooked. In welcoming them, we may be welcoming Christ himself.

When I arrived in Hastings, I realized our congregation did not reflect the growing diversity of our community. Fourteen percent of the town was Hispanic or Latino, yet on Sunday mornings our pews remained overwhelmingly Anglo. Hebrews' command to show hospitality to strangers challenged me. Were we living into the fullness of God's kingdom, or were we comfortable staying among our own?

Our first experiment was simple: Spanish classes. We thought we were learning verbs and vocabulary, but what we were really learning was how to extend ourselves toward our neighbors. When Berta began teaching, it wasn't just language—it was stories, laughter, and friendships. Soon, her friends joined us as tutors. We thought we were students, but in truth, we were hosts and guests at the same time.

Then came the folkloric dancers, filling our fellowship hall with color, music, and movement. Their practice sessions became a bridge between cultures. When they later danced in worship, our sanctuary came alive in ways we had never experienced before. Our potlucks became bilingual family reunions where tamales and casseroles sat side-by-side.

And then came Beto's taco truck. What began as a practical parking lot partnership became a ministry of hospitality. Our asphalt turned into a gathering place where strangers shared food, laughter, and conversation around picnic tables under the old elm tree. Some came for tacos but found community. In those moments, the church was not just a building but a table set wide for all.

Hebrews tells us that in welcoming strangers, we may be entertaining angels without knowing it. I have come to believe that is true. Sometimes the angel looks like a folkloric dancer twirling in ribbons, sometimes like a Spanish teacher with a radiant smile, sometimes like a taco chef handing you a plate of carne asada. Each encounter becomes a glimpse of God's kingdom, a reminder that Christ often comes to us disguised as a neighbor.

Hospitality has changed us. It has reminded us that the church is most alive when it is porous, when its walls are thin and its doors wide open. We may still wrestle with difference and stumble in our efforts, but every time we say yes to the stranger, we say yes to Jesus. And in that yes, mutual love continues.

Chapter 5

Period Poverty and Tampon Tuesdays

Breaking Taboos with Grace

"There is no longer Jew or Greek, there is no longer slave or free, there is no longer male and female; for all of you are one in Christ Jesus."

—Gal 3:28 (NRSV)

In November 2017, I had just passed the nine-month mark as pastor of First Presbyterian Church of Hastings. Being a pastor in the age of social media, I received lots of friend requests from my new church members. I would accept those requests and then spend a little bit of time scanning their profiles to learn about them. Some of them posted photos of their families, Scripture verses, and cute cat videos, while others seemed to be more politically active, at least in their social media posts.

Two of those social media profiles stuck out to me. Margaret had a profile picture wearing a beanie and protesting the Keystone XL Pipeline and some of the policies that were being passed in the new administration. Kim had a profile picture in the ubiquitous red hat with the white writing and an American flag. I learned that both of these women grew up in the church and were classmates in high school. Now they were both in their 50s and had extremely divergent political views. When I read some of their social media posts, I saw them supporting the partisan causes they cared about, defending their positions, and questioning the positions of others, sometimes passionately.

I observed these two for a few months as they occasionally engaged in animated exchanges with each other. I received an email from one of them, asking to schedule a meeting with both of them to "discuss an issue." There was no other context to the email, so I was pretty sure that I would be mediating a conflict between two church members, a task I did not feel particularly well-equipped to do.

The day of our meeting arrived and I was nervous. My palms were sweating, and I had knots in my stomach. I kept thinking about the best way to manage this meeting: should I have them sit across from each other or next to each other at the table in my office?

When they arrived, Margaret and Kim were already deep in conversation, gesturing animatedly as they walked into my office. I braced myself for a tense discussion about some theological or political controversy. Instead, they both sat down, almost in unison, and Kim began, "Pastor, we need your help."

They had both read the same article about the Pine Ridge Reservation in South Dakota, just a few hours north of us. The piece detailed the harsh realities faced by residents of Pine Ridge, particularly the women and girls. Among the many challenges was the lack of access to feminine hygiene products. This issue wasn't just about physical health; it was about dignity, education, and equality. Girls were missing school because they didn't have the supplies they needed. Some were forced to use unsanitary alternatives, putting their health at risk.

"We have to do something," Kim said, her voice passionate. "These girls deserve better. We're a church. If we're not willing to help, who will?"

Margaret nodded in agreement. "It's unacceptable," she said firmly. "I can't imagine my daughters missing school over something like this. We're in a position to help and we should."

Their unity on this issue surprised me, but it also inspired me. These two women, who seemed to disagree on nearly everything else, were coming together for a common cause. It was a reminder of the power of shared humanity and the ways in which Jesus calls us to care for "the least of these."

Margaret and Kim already had a plan. They proposed launching a drive to collect feminine hygiene products for the girls at Pine Ridge. They wanted to involve the entire church and the wider community, creating a ripple effect of awareness and action. They even had a name: "Tampon Tuesdays." I hesitated at the name. While I appreciated the alliteration and understood the humor behind it, I worried it might detract from the seriousness of the cause, and I wasn't looking forward to announcing this new mission project from the pulpit with that name. "How about we just call it the 'Feminine Hygiene Products Drive'?" I suggested. Margaret and Kim looked at each other, shrugged, and agreed. With that settled, we got to work.

The first step was raising awareness. Margaret and Kim wrote a joint article for the church newsletter, explaining the need and inviting members to donate products or funds. We announced the drive during Sunday worship, and Margaret and Kim shared their passion for the project, answering questions and encouraging participation. The response was overwhelming. Within weeks, our fellowship hall began to fill with boxes of tampons, pads, and other hygiene products. Monetary donations poured in as well. Church members who hadn't participated in a mission project in years stepped up to help sort and pack the supplies. By the end of that first drive, we had collected enough products to fill two enormous boxes, which we shipped to Pine Ridge along with a check for $1,500. Margaret and Kim beamed with pride as they helped load the boxes. Despite their political differences, they had worked together seamlessly, united by their shared commitment to making a difference.

The success of the feminine hygiene products drive sparked something bigger. It opened the door for deeper conversations about poverty, education, and justice. During a follow-up mission committee meeting, Kim shared statistics about period poverty and its impact on girls worldwide. Margaret, in turn, talked about the importance of stewardship and finding sustainable ways to support those in need.

These conversations weren't always easy. Margaret and Kim still disagreed on many issues, and their discussions could become heated. But their shared experiences working on the drive gave them a foundation of mutual respect. They learned to listen to each other, to find common ground even in the midst of disagreement.

The drive also strengthened our congregation's sense of purpose. It reminded us that mission work isn't just about writing checks or donating goods: it's about building relationships, both within our church and with the broader community. By working together, we could make a tangible difference in the lives of others while also growing in our faith and understanding.

One of the most powerful lessons from this experience was the importance of meeting people where they are. The girls at Pine Ridge didn't need lectures or charity; they needed practical help. By addressing a specific, urgent need, we were able to make a real impact. And in doing so, we learned to see these girls not as distant strangers but as our neighbors, worthy of dignity and love.

Another lesson was the value of collaboration. Margaret and Kim's partnership showed us that political and ideological differences don't have to be barriers to working together. When we focus on what unites us—our shared humanity, our faith, and our desire to make the world a better place—we can accomplish incredible things.

Finally, this experience taught us the importance of humility. None of us had all the answers, and none of us could do it alone. We had to rely on each other, on our community, and on God. In the process, we discovered that mission work isn't just about helping others; it's about being transformed ourselves.

Since that first drive, collections like these have become an ongoing ministry at First Presbyterian Church. The project has expanded beyond Pine Ridge; we now distribute supplies to local schools, shelters, and food banks, ensuring that girls and women in our own community have access to what they need.

Margaret and Kim remain the heart of the effort. They still disagree on Facebook, often vocally, but their work together has deepened their friendship. They've become an example of what it means to seek common ground in an age of polarization, showing that even in our differences, we can find ways to serve together.

The story of "Tampon Tuesdays" reminds us that a shared mission can unite us and that mission doesn't have to be grand or complicated to be meaningful. It starts with seeing a need, feeling a nudge from the Holy Spirit, and taking a step forward. It's about saying, "Yes, we can do something," even if that something feels small. And it's about trusting that God can use our efforts to make waves far beyond what we can imagine.

In moments like these, we catch glimpses of what's possible. We see the power of unity, the beauty of diversity, and the hope that comes from working together for a common cause. We see, in Margaret and Kim, in the girls at Pine Ridge, and in ourselves, the truth of Paul's words in Gal 3:28:

"There is no longer Jew or Greek, there is no longer slave or free, there is no longer male and female; for all of you are one in Christ Jesus." Even in our diverse church and our divided world, there is always room for connection, for compassion, and for hope.

Discussion Questions:

1. Margaret and Kim came together despite their differing political ideologies to address a significant need. How does their story illustrate the potential for shared goals to bridge political or ideological divides?
2. The original name for their initiative, "Tampon Tuesdays," was nixed by the pastor. How does the naming of a project influence its reception and participation? How do we balance humor or boldness with sensitivity in community initiatives?
3. The chapter describes how the drive supported girls' education on the Pine Ridge Reservation. What does this story teach us about how small, local efforts can have a significant ripple effect on broader issues?
4. Even though Margaret and Kim continue to publicly disagree on social media, they collaborated effectively on this initiative. What lessons can we take from their ability to separate personal disagreements from collective action?
5. The feminine hygiene drive became a sustained effort with significant contributions over time. What strategies or conditions might help other church or community projects achieve similar longevity and impact?

Reflection on Gal 3:28 and Chapter 5

When Paul writes to the Galatians, "There is no longer Jew or Greek, there is no longer slave or free, there is no longer male and female; for all of you are one in Christ Jesus," he is proclaiming one of the most radical visions of unity in the New Testament. In a world structured by divisions—ethnic, social, economic, and gendered—Paul insists that the cross has torn down those barriers. In Christ, we are no longer defined by what separates us but by the love that unites us.

That vision can feel lofty until you see it lived out in ordinary ways. For me, it came to life in 2017 through two church members, Margaret and Kim. On social media, they appeared to embody the very polarization tearing at the fabric of our nation: one posting about environmental protests, the other in a red hat supporting the new administration. I braced myself when they asked for a meeting, expecting conflict. Instead, I found them animated not by division but by compassion. They had both read about the struggles faced by girls on the Pine Ridge Reservation and wanted our church to respond.

Together, they launched a feminine hygiene product drive. Week by week, donations piled up in our fellowship hall: boxes of tampons, pads, supplies, and checks. Members who normally avoided mission projects pitched in. Margaret and Kim, so different in politics, stood shoulder-to-shoulder, packing boxes and celebrating the generosity of our congregation.

What happened was bigger than supplies for Pine Ridge. Their partnership gave us a glimpse of the church at its best: not erasing difference but transcending it through shared mission. They still disagree on many things, but their friendship became a testimony to Paul's vision. In Christ, the categories that divide us do not disappear, but they no longer define us.

Galatians 3:28 does not promise a world without difference. It promises a new identity that is deeper than difference: one body, bound in Christ. And every time the church steps into shared mission, whether feeding the hungry, welcoming the stranger, or standing with the vulnerable, we clothe ourselves in that truth. We live as if Paul's words are already real. Because in Christ, they are.

Chapter 6

Building Bonds While Feeding Our Hungry Neighbors

If a brother or sister is naked and lacks daily food, and one of you says to them, 'Go in peace; keep warm and eat your fill', and yet you do not supply their bodily needs, what is the good of that?

—*Isaiah 2:15–16 (NRSV)*

The first time I walked into the gym in the community center building across the street from the church on a mobile food pantry day, I was struck by the transformation. What had been an ordinary, quiet space of recreation and fellowship was now a bustling hub of life and hope. Rows of tables overflowed with fresh produce, canned goods, bread, dairy products, and pantry staples, carefully arranged to resemble a grocery store. Volunteers moved briskly, their faces bright with purpose, welcoming a steady stream of guests from the community.

Each month, a truck arrives from Omaha carrying approximately 35,000 pounds of food. The church gym, normally a place of recreation and fellowship, becomes a vibrant distribution center serving over four hundred families, sometimes more, who come seeking a food box distribution that is the equivalent of about one week's worth of groceries. No questions are asked; no qualifications required. This is simply a ministry of compassion: food for those who are hungry.

The people who come through our doors reflect the rich tapestry of our community. Among them are immigrants and refugees who have left behind everything familiar in search of safety and opportunity. They come with hope but also with uncertainty and fear. There are working poor families who work multiple jobs but still struggle to pay rent and utilities. Elderly neighbors living on fixed incomes walk in quietly, grateful for a little relief. There are those who are homeless or precariously housed, and, yes, a few who may be taking advantage of the system, but we choose to hold space for all.

One South Sudanese mother comes each month with a few of her children. She speaks little English but radiates gratitude. For her, the pantry is a lifeline, providing staples she cannot always find elsewhere. A Hispanic couple, both juggling low-wage jobs, arrive with their young son. They share their struggles quietly but appreciate the dignity with which they are treated. An elderly gentleman uses a walker and is grateful for the assistance provided by a volunteer pulling a wagon with his food box distribution in it. These stories, and countless others, remind us that hunger transcends background, politics, and circumstance.

This ministry is a beautiful example of partnership in action. Before I arrived, First Presbyterian Church joined hands with First United Methodist Church to launch the mobile food pantry. Two congregations, different in worship style and tradition, united by a common calling to serve hungry neighbors.

Every month, volunteers from both churches, along with volunteers from other churches and many local community members, come together to receive, sort, and distribute food. It is a powerful reminder that shared mission can break down walls of division.

Beyond the churches, local businesses, civic groups, and generous donors contribute to the ministry. Volunteers range widely from retirees who have the time and energy to serve, to college students eager to give back, to parents bringing their children to model service. Some volunteers once received help themselves and now seek to pay it forward.

Our mobile food pantry ministry exists at the crossroads of some of the most polarizing issues today: welfare policy, food assistance programs like SNAP, immigration, and economic inequality. These topics often spark intense debates, sometimes within our own congregation. But remarkably, the pantry has not become a source of division; instead, it has united us.

Within the congregation, views vary widely: some advocate for stricter immigration laws and reduced government assistance, others for expanded social safety nets and comprehensive immigration reform. In many contexts, these differences might be cause for conflict. Here, we have chosen a different path: focusing on what unites us—feeding hungry neighbors—rather than what divides us.

We acknowledge that welfare and immigration policies are important and complex. But as followers of Christ, we have decided that addressing the urgent need of hunger comes first. As James writes, "If a brother or sister is naked and lacks daily food, and one of you says to them, 'Go in peace; keep warm and eat your fill,' and yet you do not supply their bodily needs, what is the good of that?" (James 2:15–16).

By choosing to feed hungry neighbors regardless of their background, we embody the heart of the gospel. This is not a political act but a spiritual act of mercy and justice.

I often reflect on Maria, a single mother of three who fled violence in Guatemala. When she first came to the pantry, she was shy and unsure, struggling to navigate a new culture and language. Over time, she grew comfortable with the volunteers, who greeted her warmly and listened patiently. Eventually Maria didn't just come for the food assistance; she found belonging. This ministry became more than food; it became a community of care.

Another volunteer shared, "Seeing how much people appreciate a simple box of groceries humbles me. It reminds me that all of us are connected. None of us can do it alone."

Feeding the hungry is about more than filling stomachs. Hunger isolates, breeds shame, and deepens despair. When the church opens its doors with generosity and grace, it restores dignity and breaks down barriers. On pantry days, the atmosphere is warm and welcoming. Volunteers chat with guests, children play nearby, and neighbors connect. Relationships grow across languages, cultures, and economic divides. This ministry is as much about hospitality as it is about food distribution. The mobile food pantry is a place where love takes tangible form in serving neighbors in need.

Running a mobile food pantry is a complex undertaking. Coordinating deliveries, managing volunteers, ensuring food safety, and respecting guests' privacy require constant attention. Funding can be uncertain, and the needs of the community are always evolving.

Flexibility has been essential. Transportation can be a barrier for some, so we have explored partnerships to improve access. The COVID-19 pandemic dramatically altered how we did the distribution, but we never missed a month. Now, rather than our neighbors coming into the building and going through the gym to collect their distribution, we deliver it to their cars. We have lost some of the relational aspect of the ministry due to this change; however, we are still feeding our neighbors and sharing the love of Christ in tangible ways.

Above all, the greatest lesson has been the power of focusing on common purpose rather than division. In a polarized world, the simple act of feeding hungry neighbors is a radical witness to the gospel's unifying power.

Throughout Scripture, God's heart for the hungry and marginalized is unmistakable.

The prophet Isaiah challenges God's people:

> Is not this the fast that I choose:
> to loose the bonds of injustice,
> to undo the thongs of the yoke,
> to let the oppressed go free,
> and to break every yoke?
> Is it not to share your bread with the hungry,
> and bring the homeless poor into your house;
> when you see the naked, to cover them. (Isa 58:6–7 NRSV)

Jesus, echoing these themes, identifies with the hungry and the stranger in Matt 25: "Truly I tell you, just as you did it to one of the least of these who are members of my family, you did it to me."

This ministry embodies the essence of these passages. Feeding the hungry is not optional for the church; it is an integral expression of faith; it is a glimpse of the kingdom of God.

In addition to the unity and sense of purpose this mobile food pantry distribution has given our church, there is an added and unintentional benefit of church growth. Members of our church have invited their friends to come and volunteer with the food distribution. As they have come back month after month to do so, some of those volunteers have become more interested in the church. They see a church that is trying to "walk the walk," and so they start attending worship and participating in other programs at the church. Almost every new member's class that I have taught in the last eight years has included at least one individual or family who came to know our church through volunteering at the food distribution. While this was not a stated goal of this ministry, it has become a beautiful unintended consequence that has grown our church in numbers and in witness.

Our work in Hastings is an earthly echo of that heavenly vision. Each bag of groceries, each moment of hospitality, participates in God's redeeming work in the world. As I reflect on the mobile food pantry, I am filled with gratitude and hope. This ministry is a living testimony to what a community can do when love and faith guide action. Our prayer is that the ministry continues to grow, that new volunteers and donors are inspired to join, and that the pantry adapts to meet changing community needs.

This ministry reminds us that in feeding hungry neighbors, we not only meet physical needs but also bear witness to the love of Christ in a fractured world.

Discussion Questions

1. How does the mobile food pantry ministry reflect the call of Jesus to feed the hungry and welcome the stranger? Can you identify similar ministries in your community?
2. What are some ways your congregation or community can rise above political or cultural divisions to serve a common need?
3. How can the church balance the importance of advocating for systemic change with the immediate work of meeting physical needs?
4. Reflect on a time you were part of a ministry that brought together people with differing views or backgrounds. What made it successful or challenging?
5. How does serving neighbors in need shape your own understanding of faith and community?

Reflection on Isaiah 2:15–16 and Chapter 6

James is blunt. If a brother or sister is hungry or without clothing, and we respond with kind words but no tangible help, "what is the good of that?" Words of blessing without acts of mercy are empty. Real faith is not abstract belief or polite sentiment—it is embodied in action that meets the real needs of neighbors.

I think of these verses every time I walk into the gym on mobile food pantry day. What was once an ordinary space of basketball games and fellowship becomes a sanctuary of compassion. Tables overflow with bread, milk, vegetables, and staples. Volunteers welcome neighbors as if they were old friends. The energy is not transactional but relational, rooted in dignity and hope.

On those days, James' words come alive. We are not saying, "Go in peace, keep warm, eat your fill." We are, quite literally, handing out food so that families can eat their fill. And yet, as powerful as the groceries are, the true gift is something deeper: the gift of being seen, of being welcomed without condition, of knowing that you belong.

The ministry is not without complexity. Volunteers hold different political views. Some advocate for expanded social programs, others for personal responsibility and smaller government. National debates about welfare or immigration could divide us. But on pantry days, none of that matters. We are united by a higher calling: to feed the hungry, because Christ first fed us.

Each person who comes through the line carries a story: the South Sudanese mother who radiates gratitude, the elderly neighbor leaning on a walker, the single mother from Guatemala finding her way in a new land. Each one is a reminder that hunger knows no boundaries. Each one is a living testimony to the truth James insists upon: faith without works is dead.

In a fractured world, the pantry offers a glimpse of God's kingdom. It is a place where faith and works come together, where love takes the form of groceries, wagons, and handshakes, where neighbors become family. It is a reminder that the gospel is not only something we proclaim but something we practice, one box of food at a time.

Chapter 7

Quilting Confessionals

Stories Stitched in Faith

As God's chosen ones, holy and beloved, clothe yourselves with compassion, kindness, humility, meekness, and patience. Bear with one another and, if anyone has a complaint against another, forgive each other; just as the Lord has forgiven you, so you also must forgive. Above all, clothe yourselves with love, which binds everything together in perfect harmony.

—Col3:12–14 (NRSV)

Every Tuesday at 1 p.m., the quilting room in our church's community center fills with the tapping of a needle sliding up and down, the soft rustle of fabric, and the steady rhythm of scissors clipping threads. This is the sacred hour when the church's quilting circle gathers. It's a tradition that has been alive for decades, but in recent years, it has taken on a new significance as a space where faith, friendship, and the messy realities of life intersect.

The quilting circle is made up of a group of women from all walks of life. Some are long-time members of the church, others relatively new; some lean conservative, others liberal; some are retired, others are full-time mothers and grandmothers. Their quilts are as diverse as their stories;

patchworks of colors, textures, and patterns that reflect the complexity and beauty of their lives.

On any given Tuesday, the circle might be stitching together a quilt for a newborn baby shower, a fundraiser for the church's mission trips, a military quilt to be given at a special ceremony, or a special memorial quilt for a family who has lost a loved one. But the quilts are more than just fabric and thread. They are the backdrop to conversations that weave together laughter, tears, disagreement, confession, and grace.

The quilting circle began decades ago as a simple ministry: women gathering to create comforting blankets for those in need. Over time, it evolved into something deeper: a safe space for connection and conversation in a community marked by increasing polarization.

The women of the quilting circle represent a wide spectrum of political beliefs, social backgrounds, and life experiences. This diversity could be a recipe for conflict. Yet, remarkably, these women manage to maintain a respectful, civil dialogue week after week. It's not because everyone agrees on everything—in fact, they often don't—but because they share a commitment to listen and learn from one another.

There's "Marge," a lifelong Republican and retired pastor's wife who moved to Hastings in retirement. She's outspoken and passionate, never afraid to voice her opinions. Then there's "Sarah," a young mother who grew up in the church with two children who often come and play in the quilting room. Sarah sometimes challenges Marge's views but always with curiosity rather than confrontation.

"You learn that the quilt isn't about the fabric you pick but how you sew the pieces together," Marge once told me. "It's a good metaphor for life—and for this group."

The circle's ability to engage respectfully in difficult conversations is no accident. It is cultivated, nurtured, and intentional. These women have learned the art of "quilted confessionals," a term I use to describe the way they share their stories honestly, admit their mistakes, and hold space for others to do the same.

During a recent gathering, the conversation turned to a contentious political issue that had been dividing the community. Voices were raised, opinions stated strongly, and for a moment, tension crackled in the air. Then "Linda," a retired schoolteacher, paused the discussion with a simple reminder: "We're here to listen, not to convince."

That moment shifted the tone. Women began sharing personal stories about why they felt the way they did: stories of family struggles, hopes for their children, fears about the future. These stories weren't arguments; they were windows into each other's lives.

It reminded me of Jesus' call to love one another, not just as abstract theology but as a radical practice. These women were embodying that call. They weren't ignoring their differences; they were inviting those differences into a space of grace and respect.

Each quilt tells a story. Some are carefully planned from start to finish, with each square chosen for its meaning. Others come together more spontaneously, with scraps from old clothes, curtains, or fabric donated by church members. But all are testimonies to the faith and life of the makers.

One quilt I saw recently was made for a veteran in the congregation. The squares included fabric from military uniforms, patches from deployment locations, and colors that symbolized hope and healing. The quilt was a tapestry of history and prayer, stitched with care by a team of women who understood the veteran's sacrifice.

Another quilt was made from baby clothes of children born in the church community, sewn by mothers who had grown up in the quilting circle themselves. That quilt wasn't just a gift: it was a blessing, a tangible sign of the ongoing life of the church.

These quilts remind us that faith is lived in tangible acts of care and craftsmanship. They are symbols of hope, healing, and the beauty of diversity stitched into unity.

What does quilting have to do with finding common ground in the age of polarization? More than you might think. The act of quilting, taking diverse pieces and joining them together into a unified whole, is a powerful metaphor for our call to unity as the body of Christ.

In the New Testament, Paul writes in Eph 4:16, "From him the whole body, joined and held together by every supporting ligament, grows and builds itself up in love, as each part does its work." The quilting circle embodies this truth. Each woman brings her unique piece, and together they create something greater than the sum of its parts.

Quilting also reflects the gospel message of reconciliation and restoration. Broken pieces of fabric, discarded scraps, are transformed into something beautiful and useful. Similarly, the church is called to be a community where brokenness is met with grace and where diversity is a source of strength, not division.

The quilting circle is more than just a weekly gathering. It's a ministry that reaches beyond the church walls. The quilts made are given to those in need: people experiencing homelessness, families in crisis, newborns in the hospital, veterans recovering from trauma. Each quilt carries with it prayers for healing, comfort, and hope. When a quilt is wrapped around someone's shoulders, it is a physical reminder that they are not alone, that their community cares deeply.

This ministry also provides a model for how faith can engage with a polarized world. It doesn't require everyone to agree on politics or ideology. Instead, it invites us to focus on shared humanity, to listen deeply, and to work together for the common good.

Over the years, I've learned many lessons from the quilting circle that apply far beyond their weekly meetings:

1. Shared purpose creates unity: When people come together around a common goal—whether making quilts or serving a community need—they can overcome differences that might otherwise divide them.

2. Civil disagreement is possible: You don't have to agree on everything to maintain respect and kindness. Listening to stories, not just opinions, builds empathy.

3. The whole is greater than the parts: diversity is a gift. Different perspectives and experiences can enrich a community when embraced with humility and grace.

4. Tangible acts matter: faith isn't just about ideas; it's about action. Small acts of care, like sewing a quilt, can have profound spiritual and communal impact.

5. Transformation is mutual: ministry changes not only those who receive but also those who give. The quilting circle members have grown in their faith and understanding through their shared work.

The quilting circle is not without its challenges. Occasionally, strong disagreements surface and personalities clash. Sometimes, political tensions seep in despite everyone's best efforts. There have been moments when members considered leaving the group out of frustration or hurt. But each time, the group recommits to their shared values of respect and grace. They remind one another that the goal isn't to change minds but to build relationships and to embody Christ's love in a fractured world. Their persistence gives me hope. It shows that even in our polarized culture, there are places where unity and civility are possible and places where people can quilt together, in both fabric and spirit.

As I reflect on the quilting circle, I see a microcosm of the church universal. We are all pieces of a larger tapestry: different colors, shapes, and textures, called to be joined together in love. The quilting circle teaches us that faith is not about uniformity but unity. It is about embracing difference and holding it gently with humility and grace. It is about listening deeply to one another's stories and letting those stories shape us. In a world that too often seems defined by division, the quilting circle offers a different way, a way of stitching together hope, grace, and community, one patch at a time.

Discussion Questions:

1. The quilting circle includes women from a wide range of political and social backgrounds who often disagree yet work together. What does their story teach us about the possibility of civil discourse and respectful disagreement within faith communities today?
2. How does the metaphor of quilting—bringing diverse pieces together to create a unified whole—apply to your experience of church, community, or society? What challenges and opportunities does this metaphor present?
3. The quilting circle's ministry involves creating tangible gifts that express care and prayer. In what ways can physical acts of service deepen spiritual connections in your own faith context?
4. What are some practical ways your church or community might create "quilted confessionals" or safe spaces for honest, respectful conversation across differences?
5. The quilting circle demonstrates how ministry changes both the giver and the receiver. How have you experienced mutual transformation in your own acts of service or community engagement?

Reflection on Col3:12–14 and Chapter 7

Paul's exhortation to the Colossians is both beautiful and practical: "As God's chosen ones, holy and beloved, clothe yourselves with compassion, kindness, humility, meekness, and patience. Bear with one another … forgive each other … and above all, clothe yourselves with love, which binds everything together in perfect harmony." These words remind us that Christian faith is not simply a matter of belief but of embodiment. We are called to wear these virtues the way we wear clothing, so that they shape not only our inner life but the way we are seen and experienced by others.

Every Tuesday at 1 p.m., the quilting room in our church's community center becomes a living parable of these verses. Women of different ages, backgrounds, and political perspectives gather with needles, scissors, and fabric in hand. At first glance, it looks like a hobby group. But if you stay long enough, you realize it is something much deeper: a community stitched together by compassion, patience, humility, and, above all, love.

These women do not always agree. Sometimes their conversations circle around contentious issues. At times, tempers flare or disagreements emerge. Yet again and again, they choose to bear with one another, to listen rather than convince, to forgive and move forward. In doing so, they model what Paul is urging: that we clothe ourselves not with pride or anger but with virtues that allow us to stay in relationship, even when it is hard.

The quilts they make are metaphors in fabric. Scraps that might seem useless on their own are joined together into something beautiful and whole. Likewise, the body of Christ is a patchwork of diverse lives and stories, bound together by the thread of God's love. Each quilt becomes a testimony to the truth Paul proclaims: love is what holds everything together in harmony.

When one of these quilts is placed around the shoulders of a veteran, or laid on the lap of a grieving family, or given to a newborn, it is more than warmth. It is a tangible sign of the gospel, a reminder that we are never alone, that God's people surround us with care.

In a polarized world, the quilting circle shows us what it means to be clothed with love. It is not about erasing differences or stitching only with matching fabrics. It is about bringing together what is varied, even frayed, and letting love be the thread that binds it all.

Chapter 8

Gun Violence, Youth Leadership, and Prayer

Rejoice in hope, be patient in suffering, persevere in prayer. Contribute to the needs of the saints; extend hospitality to strangers. Bless those who persecute you; bless and do not curse them. Rejoice with those who rejoice, weep with those who weep.

—Rom 12:12–15 (NRSV)

When I moved to Nebraska in March 2017 to begin my ministry at First Presbyterian Church of Hastings, I came with a heart full of hope and the idealism that often accompanies a new pastoral call. I believed in the possibilities of building bridges across difference, of shepherding a congregation committed to service and compassion, and of seeking the common good in a time of growing political polarization. I still believe in those things. But it didn't take long before I was confronted with a harsh reality that followed me from my previous contexts and made itself tragically present in Nebraska too: the devastating epidemic of gun violence in America and the contentious political debate around gun control.

Between March 2017 and March 2018, my first twelve months in Hastings, there were eighty-two mass shootings in the United States that resulted in two or more fatalities. These shootings claimed the lives of 342 people. Those numbers are staggering, but they fail to convey the depth of grief, trauma, and fear that ripple out from each act of violence, affecting families, schools, neighborhoods, and entire communities.

Some of these tragedies dominated headlines and entered into the consciousness of our local community: the massacre at the Route 91 Harvest Festival in Las Vegas that left fifty-eight dead and hundreds more injured; the shooting at the First Baptist Church in Sutherland Springs, Texas, where twenty-six worshipers were killed; and the horror of the Parkland school shooting on Valentine's Day 2018, when seventeen students and staff at Marjory Stoneman Douglas High School were gunned down. Other shootings barely registered in the national consciousness, each one a life-shattering event for the people involved, even if it didn't make the evening news.

As a pastor, I felt the weight of these tragedies not just as a citizen or a parent but as a spiritual leader entrusted with guiding a congregation through grief, anger, and moral reflection. I began changing the marquee sign outside our church building after each high-profile shooting: "Pray for Las Vegas," "Pray for Sutherland Springs," "Pray for Parkland." There was one week that we had multiple mass shootings, so I changed the sign to read "Pray for victims of gun violence." It was a simple gesture, one small way to acknowledge the pain and ask our community to pause in solidarity with the grieving. But even that small gesture stirred a surprising amount of controversy.

The week I put up that sign, a member approached me, visibly upset. "Pastor, when you put those signs up, it feels like you're making a political statement," he said. "I'm tired of people blaming guns instead of the people who misuse them." This church member told me that he had been approached by other community members who were also offended by our church signs. I tried to explain to him that due to the scope and magnitude of the mass shootings last week, there wasn't enough room on our signboard for me to list out each city. I asked him, "Have we become so polarized that a request for prayer for a particular group of people who have experienced a particular form of trauma is now considered political or inappropriate?" I explained that the signboard is not advocating for banning guns or proposing a policy solution; it is inviting prayer for a particular group of people who are victims of a particular trauma. The church member left, and I could sense his frustration.

A few days later, another member pulled me aside in the grocery store. "Thank you for those signs," he said. "It's important to name what's happening in our country and not pretend we're immune just because we live in Nebraska."

Those two comments, in the span of a week, captured what it means to lead a purple church in a red state. Even something as seemingly neutral as praying for the victims of mass shootings had become a political Rorschach test.

Still, I believe that faith communities must find ways to engage with the grief and horror of gun violence without being paralyzed by partisan politics. We are called to mourn with those who mourn. We are called to seek peace. And we are called to bear witness to the value of every human life.

After the Parkland shooting in February of 2018, something shifted in the national conversation. The students at Marjory Stoneman Douglas refused to let their classmates die in vain. They organized protests. They held press conferences. They lobbied lawmakers and flooded the streets of Washington, DC, for the March for Our Lives. Their courage and clarity inspired a generation, and their energy was contagious, even in communities like ours.

A few weeks after the shooting, several members of our church's youth group approached me. "Pastor Greg," one of them said, "we want to do something. We're tired of just watching the news and feeling helpless." I was moved by their urgency and their vulnerability. They were asking for guidance, but they were also offering leadership. These were not kids parroting talking points from cable news; they were young people trying to make sense of the world and their place in it.

We gathered one evening and talked openly. Some of them wanted to organize a protest march. Others wanted to write letters to our representatives. A few worried that any kind of action might stir controversy in our community. I listened, then shared a proposal: What if we organized a prayer vigil on April 20, the anniversary of the Columbine shooting? What if we invited the entire community? We weren't going to gather to argue policy but to grieve, to pray, and to stand together in hope. There was a moment of silence. Then, slowly, nods around the room. "Yes," one of them said. "That's something everyone could come to. We need that."

After my experience with the signboard messages, I knew that even something as seemingly uncontroversial as a prayer vigil could be divisive.

So before moving forward, I picked up the phone and began calling church members I knew to be strong supporters of the Second Amendment: people who owned guns, hunted regularly, or had spoken out in favor of gun rights in the past. I didn't call them to ask permission. I called to share the vision and to listen.

"I want to hold a prayer vigil," I told them. "It's not going to be political. We're not going to advocate for specific policies or invite elected officials to speak. We're going to name the grief that so many of us feel, light candles, sing hymns, read Scripture, and pray for healing. Is this something you can support, and would you be willing to come?"

To my relief, and honestly, to my surprise, every single one of them said they could support this. One even offered to help coordinate logistics. "I may not agree with everything folks are saying about guns right now," he said, "but I agree with you about the need to pray." Their willingness to engage made all the difference. It reminded me that when you lead with empathy, when you invite people into something larger than the culture wars, many will show up with open hearts.

On April 20, 2018, our sanctuary filled with people. Presbyterians, Episcopalians, United Church of Christ members, Disciples of Christ members, Baptists, and unaffiliated neighbors who had heard about the vigil through word of mouth or Facebook showed up.

We began with silence; a long, aching silence broken only by the lighting of candles. We read the names and ages of the victims from Columbine, Sandy Hook, and Parkland. For each name, a bell tolled. For each child, tears were shed.

We sang "Amazing Grace," we heard Scripture passages that speak to the brokenness of our world and the hope for something better: Isaiah's vision of swords turned into plowshares, Jesus' words from the Sermon on the Mount, Paul's call to overcome evil with good.

One local pastor read a reflection on the Hebrew word "shalom," not just peace as the absence of conflict but peace as the presence of wholeness, justice, and right relationship. We prayed, not just for the victims and their families but for our nation. We prayed for lawmakers and teachers, for first responders and grieving parents, for perpetrators and survivors.

I offered a short prayer of lament. "In the Bible," I said, "lament is not the opposite of faith; it's a form of faith. It's what God's people do when the world isn't as it should be. It's how we hold our pain before God and say, 'This is not okay. We are not okay. Help us.'"

At the close of the vigil, we invited each attendee to come forward and light a candle at the communion table. Hundreds of flames flickered in the dim sanctuary, each one a prayer, each one a cry for peace.

In the days that followed, I heard from many who attended the vigil. A high school teacher thanked me for including students. A grandmother said she hadn't been to church for a while but came that afternoon because "my soul needed it." One of the gun rights advocates I had spoken with beforehand told me quietly, "Thank you for making space where I didn't feel attacked. I may not agree with everyone here, but I felt God's presence today."

That was the moment I knew we had done something holy. Not because we had solved the problem of gun violence. Not because we had passed new legislation or drafted bold manifestos. But because we had made space for grief. Because we had shown that it's possible to come together across political lines and say, with one voice, "This is not the way it's supposed to be." That is the unique role faith communities can play. Not as echo chambers of political ideology but as sanctuaries for moral courage. As places where it's safe to feel, to question, to mourn, and to hope.

Of course, one vigil does not fix what is broken. In 2018 alone, the year of our vigil, there were 340 mass shootings in the United States, nearly one per day according to the Gun Violence Archive. Those shootings resulted in 373 deaths and over 1,300 injuries.

What should the church be doing in the face of such a crisis? We can pray, yes. But we must also act. For some congregations, that may mean hosting educational forums about gun safety and mental health. For others, it might involve partnering with local law enforcement on gun buyback programs or offering trauma-informed care to victims of violence. In our case, we began with the vigil, but we didn't stop there. Our youth continued to raise their voices. They organized a march here in Hastings. Some posted on social media. Others organized a letter-writing campaign to members of Congress.

I was proud of them, not because they were pushing a particular policy but because they were living their faith out loud. Because they refused to believe that cynicism was the only option. Gun violence remains one of the most intractable and emotionally charged issues in American public life. But it is also one of the clearest places where the church is called to bear witness.

To bear witness means to speak the truth in love, even when it's unpopular.

To bear witness means to create space for grief and anger—and also for grace.

And to bear witness means to believe that even in a red state, even in a purple church, we can find common ground, not because we agree on everything but because we belong to each other.

We are members of one body, Paul writes in 1 Cor. When one member suffers, all suffer with it. Let us suffer together. And then let us rise, together, to build a world where no child has to practice active shooter drills, where no parent has to plan a funeral after a school day, where peace is not a political slogan but a lived reality.

Discussion Questions:

1. Shared Values: How can communities with diverse political beliefs find common ground in addressing issues like gun violence?
2. Role of Faith: What role should faith communities play in responding to societal crises like mass shootings?
3. Youth Engagement: How can churches empower young people to lead initiatives for justice and peace in their communities?
4. Beyond Prayer: While prayer is vital, what additional steps can faith communities take to address the root causes of gun violence?
5. Sustained Effort: How can churches maintain momentum in their advocacy work beyond the immediate aftermath of a tragedy?

Reflection on Rom 12:12–15 and Chapter 8

Paul's words to the Romans are as concise as they are demanding: "Rejoice in hope, be patient in suffering, persevere in prayer. Contribute to the needs of the saints; extend hospitality to strangers. Bless those who persecute you; bless and do not curse them. Rejoice with those who rejoice, weep with those who weep."

It is a vision of Christian community that is startling in its simplicity. Hope, patience, prayer, generosity, blessing, hospitality, solidarity. This is what it means to be the body of Christ. And yet, in a world fractured by violence and division, these commands can feel impossibly idealistic. How can we rejoice when the headlines are so heavy? How can we bless those who wound us? How can we hold joy and sorrow together when suffering is so pervasive?

Paul's answer is not a program but a posture. He calls the church to be a community marked by presence: present with God in prayer, present with neighbors in need, present with one another in joy and in sorrow. The Christian life is not about quick fixes or easy answers. It is about patient, persevering love that refuses to look away from suffering and refuses to give up hope.

I was reminded of this in my first year of ministry in Nebraska, when mass shootings dominated the news cycle with tragic regularity. Each time I changed the church sign to say "Pray for Las Vegas" or "Pray for Parkland," I was simply trying to live into Paul's words: to persevere in prayer, to name suffering, and to call my community to solidarity. Some saw those signs as political. Others saw them as pastoral. But for me, they were an act of faith, an attempt to weep with those who weep.

That posture culminated in April 2018, when our congregation, alongside others, hosted a prayer vigil on the anniversary of Columbine. We gathered not to debate policies but to bear witness to grief and to seek God's peace. We read names, we lit candles, we sang hymns. And in that holy space, something happened: people who disagreed fiercely about gun laws stood side-by-side in silence, tears on their cheeks, prayers on their lips. We discovered that lament is not the opposite of faith. It is faith. It is how we hold our brokenness before God and before one another.

That evening, I realized Paul's words are not lofty ideals but practical instructions. To rejoice in hope is not to deny suffering but to cling to the promise that suffering does not get the last word. To persevere in prayer is not to retreat into passivity but to anchor our cries for justice and peace in God's power. To weep with those who weep is not weakness but solidarity, the kind of solidarity that can carry us through unspeakable loss.

The church may not have all the answers to the epidemic of violence in our land. But we do have a calling: to show up, to keep praying, to keep blessing, to keep rejoicing and weeping together until God's vision of peace is made real. That is not partisan. That is gospel.

Chapter 9

Polemic Ponderings

Can Anything Good Come Out of Nazareth or Haiti?

The next day Jesus decided to go to Galilee. He found Philip and said to him, "Follow me." Now Philip was from Bethsaida, the city of Andrew and Peter. Philip found Nathanael and said to him, "We have found him about whom Moses in the law and also the prophets wrote, Jesus son of Joseph from Nazareth." Nathanael said to him, "Can anything good come out of Nazareth?" Philip said to him, "Come and see."

—John 1:43–46 (NRSV)

On January 12, 2018, just a few weeks before the first anniversary of my call to serve in Nebraska, news broke that President Donald Trump had referred to Haiti and African nations as "$#!%hole countries" during a bipartisan meeting about immigration policy. I had not yet made it through my first year at First Presbyterian Church of Hastings, Nebraska, a church striving to be purple in a red state, and I was still finding my footing. I didn't want to be seen as partisan. I didn't want to alienate the people who had entrusted me with their pulpit. But I also couldn't let those words go unchallenged.

They stung. Not just because of the crude language or the racism barely veiled behind it but because I knew Haiti. I had been there. I had worked alongside Haitian partners, prayed in their churches, sung their hymns, and broken bread with them. I had seen their resilience in the wake of disasters, their joy in worship, and their sacrificial compassion for neighbors. Haiti was not a "$#!%hole country." Haiti was holy ground filled with precious children of God made in the image of God. So were the other African countries that were referenced in that meeting. Referring to them that way was antithetical to the gospel we proclaim and antithetical to basic human decency.

Something had to be said, and yet, I hesitated for a moment. I didn't want to rock the boat. I prayed and I reached out to mentors of mine, including pastors serving in similar contexts. Their advice to me was direct and simple: stick to the Scriptures. There is enough material in there to use, and if you stick to the Scriptures and people want to get upset about your sermon, they will have to take it up with the Bible.

That Sunday, I had the Revised Common Lectionary (RCL) to guide me. The RCL offers a series of readings every week for pastors to use. It is on a three-year cycle that was established in the 1980s, so the text for that Sunday had been selected for me by a committee more than three decades ago. I often describe the lectionary as a pastor's best friend—and sometimes our fiercest provocateur. It encourages pastors to preach on texts they might not otherwise consider, and it provides a cohesive set of texts that tie together the Old Testament, the Psalms, a Gospel reading, and an epistle.

That week it gave me 1 Sam 3:1–10, the story of God calling out Samuel's name, and John 1:43–51, the story of Jesus calling Philip and Nathanael to become his disciples. It includes the moment when Nathanael scoffs, "Can anything good come out of Nazareth?"

Biblical scholars state that Nazareth was considered a backwater. It was a place that people mocked as being uneducated and uncivilized, and yet it produced Jesus of Nazareth. I saw the connection immediately. Ancient Nazareth was present-day Haiti. And so, I preached. I stepped into the pulpit with some fear and trembling, knowing that this could go poorly. But I trusted the text, and I trusted the stories I had brought back with me from Haiti. I didn't need to call anyone out. I just needed to lift people up.

We began with prayer: "Lord, may the words of my mouth and the meditations of all of our hearts be pleasing in your sight, our rock and redeemer. Amen." Then, I set the scene: "As I mentioned last week, we are in the Season of Epiphany. It is the time of the Christian year when we reflect on God revealing Godself to the world in Jesus Christ. We are confronted with a really interesting story in the Gospel of John this morning that starts to reveal Jesus' identity to us."

And then I zoomed in on Nathanael's question: "Can anything good come out of Nazareth?"

I told them about Nazareth. A dusty hilltop village of perhaps one hundred families. No synagogue. No paved roads. A place of peasants, laborers, and illiterate farmers. Reza Aslan calls it "inconsequential and utterly forgettable."[1] I asked the congregation if this might sound familiar? I told them Haiti might be our modern-day Nazareth. Poor. Forgotten. Devastated by natural disasters. Stereotyped. Written off.

"Can anything good come out of Haiti?" I asked. Then I shared stories. First, Dr. Jerry: "Dr. Jerry grew up on La Gonave—the forgotten part of the forgotten country. He defied all odds to finish high school, study medicine in Cuba, and return to serve the people of his home island. He could be living in Port-au-Prince or Miami, but he chooses La Gonave. Can anything good come out of Haiti? Yes. Dr. Jerry."

Then, Madame Lisson: "She runs a bakery in a rural village. With a microloan from a church, she expanded her business, employed her neighbors, and sent her children to school. She is a pillar of her community. She has a smile that lights up the world. Can anything good come out of Haiti? Yes. Madame Lisson."

Then I invited the congregation to come and see: "Come and see Haiti through my eyes. Come and see the image of God reflected in these people. Come and see what God can do with so-called backwaters."

I never explicitly mentioned the comments made in the news—I didn't have to. The connection was clear. After the service, one of the most active Republicans in our congregation came up to me. He'd served on local campaigns and was known for his conservative values. He said, "That was magnanimous. And it needed to be said." It floored me. I had expected pushback. I had prepared myself for angry emails. But what I received was gratitude. Not from everyone, of course. But from enough people to remind me that this purple church in a red state could hold space for prophetic truth, spoken in love.

There is a kind of grace in telling the truth about people others try to erase. There is power in reclaiming dignity with stories and Scripture. There is healing in finding common ground through the shared language

1. Reza Aslan, *Zealot: The Life and Times of Jesus of Nazareth* (New York: Random House, 2014), 25–26.

of faith. The sermon wasn't partisan. It was pastoral. It wasn't an attack on a president. It was a defense of precious people. And it reminded me that the church can be a place where we resist the dehumanization of others, not by shouting louder but by speaking more lovingly. Not by debating ideology but by lifting up incarnate stories. By naming the image of God in everyone, even those the world tries to forget.

We don't talk enough about the power of presence. When I was in Haiti, I wasn't there to fix anything. I was there to learn, to accompany, to be in relationship. We sat under mango trees and read Scripture. And more than anything else, we listened. And in listening, we discovered God already at work.

I remember once sitting in a circle in a one-room church with a corrugated tin roof, with chickens wandering in and out. We had just finished a devotion, and I asked one of our Haitian partners, "How can we pray for you?" He looked me in the eye and said, "Pray that we would be faithful." Not rich. Not safe. Not comfortable. Faithful. That moment shook me. Here were people who had every reason to be bitter or cynical, and instead, they prayed for faithfulness. I saw Christ in that prayer.

2018 was a year when public discourse felt especially coarse and brutal. Racial tensions were high. Polarization was deepening. And words mattered. When the president of the United States uses language that degrades entire nations and peoples, it signals permission for others to do the same. Churches, especially purple ones, often struggle with how to respond. We want to be welcoming to everyone, including those who support the president and those who oppose him. We want to be unified. But we also need to be faithful. And being faithful sometimes means stepping into uncomfortable territory.

This sermon became a turning point for me. I realized that faithfulness doesn't have to be loud or angry. It can be gentle and compelling. It can quote Scripture, tell stories, and trust that the Spirit is at work. We often think that preaching against injustice has to mean naming names and pointing fingers. But sometimes, the most powerful witness is simply inviting people to come and see: to look into the eyes of someone they thought they had figured out and discover the face of Christ.

That's what happened to Nathanael. Philip didn't try to convince him with an argument. He simply said, "Come and see." When Nathanael came, he encountered Jesus, and his assumptions fell away. That's what can happen when we take people seriously enough to tell their stories, when we lift up their lives as sacred, and when we refuse to let slurs be the final word.

Since that day, I've come back to this moment again and again. Not just when political rhetoric takes a dark turn but whenever I wonder whether preaching with conviction is worth the risk. The lesson I learned that Sunday was that if I speak from a place of love—love for Scripture, love for the people in the pews, and love for those being spoken about—people will listen. They may not agree with every word, but they will recognize the heart behind it.

And when we trust that God's word is more powerful than political soundbites, we become conduits for healing. We become truth-tellers. We become reminders that the church can still be a moral compass, not by meeting darkness with force, but by reflecting and magnifying the light.

Discussion Questions:

1. Have you ever been surprised by encountering something good in a person or place you had written off? What did that teach you?
2. How can we respond faithfully to public statements or actions that contradict our values, especially in a politically divided context?
3. What are the "Nazareths" in your life—places or people you might struggle to see God's presence in? How can you be more open to "coming and seeing"?
4. How does telling stories of human dignity, like those of Dr. Jerry and Madame Lisson, help us build common ground in polarized communities?
5. What might it look like for your church to speak truth with love in your current context? Where is God calling you to be brave and magnanimous?

Reflection on John 1:43–46 and Chapter 9

In John's Gospel, the call of the first disciples unfolds with a remarkable simplicity. Jesus finds Philip and says, "Follow me." Philip then finds Nathanael and announces, "We have found him—the one about whom Moses and the prophets wrote, Jesus of Nazareth." Nathanael's response is cutting: "Can anything good come out of Nazareth?"

It is a question laced with skepticism and prejudice. Nazareth was a small, dusty village with no reputation for producing greatness. It was a place easily dismissed, a backwater. Nathanael's scorn echoes a familiar human instinct: to write people off because of where they come from, the accent they carry, the color of their skin, or the poverty of their neighborhood.

Philip doesn't argue back. He doesn't debate. He simply says, "Come and see." And that invitation makes all the difference. Nathanael comes, he sees Jesus for himself, and his dismissive question gives way to confession: "Rabbi, you are the Son of God."

That same dynamic unfolded for me in January 2018. When the president referred to Haiti and African nations as "$#!%hole countries," it pierced me deeply because I knew those places. I had prayed in Haitian churches, sung their hymns, and shared meals with their people. I had seen their resilience and their joy, their faith and their faithfulness. They were not places to be scorned. They were holy ground.

And yet, the question hung in the air: "Can anything good come out of Haiti?" It was Nathanael's question all over again. My answer, like Philip's, was not to debate but to invite: "Come and see." Come and see Dr. Jerry, who returned to serve the forgotten island of La Gonave as a physician. Come and see Madame Lisson, whose bakery sustains her family and community. Come and see the image of God alive in people who are too often dismissed by the world.

The gospel doesn't call us to win arguments. It calls us to bear witness—to invite people to see what God is doing in unexpected places and among unexpected people. The power of Philip's words, "Come and see," is that they leave room for God to do the convincing. They create space for encounter, for revelation, for hearts to be changed not by rhetoric but by relationship.

In a divided world, where dismissive questions and degrading labels abound, the church's calling is to keep extending that invitation. "Come and see" the goodness of God in those you've written off. "Come and see" the Christ who dwells among the poor, the marginalized, and the forgotten. "Come and see" that the light shines even in the places the world calls dark.

When we dare to issue that invitation—and when we ourselves are willing to accept it—we discover again and again that grace shows up in Nazareth, in Haiti, and in every place the world devalues. And in those encounters, our skepticism is transformed into faith, our prejudice into praise, and our dismissive questions into the recognition that Christ has been among us all along.

Chapter 10

Friendship and Revival Across Faith Traditions

"I ask not only on behalf of these, but also on behalf of those who will believe in me through their word, that they may all be one. As you, Father, are in me and I am in you, may they also be in us, so that the world may believe that you have sent me. The glory that you have given me I have given them, so that they may be one, as we are one, I in them and you in me, that they may become completely one, so that the world may know that you have sent me and have loved them even as you have loved me."

—John 17:20–23 (NRSV)

In the spring of 2018, Hastings, Nebraska, was a town wrestling with both its small-town charm and its undercurrents of division. The previous year had brought waves of political and cultural tension nationwide, and even our modest community was not immune. As I shared in chapter three, in August of 2017, racist flyers had been posted around town. As the pastor of First Presbyterian Church of Hastings, I felt compelled to respond not just with a sermon or a prayer but with a public witness.

So I invited fellow clergy to join me on the steps of City Hall. It wasn't a massive demonstration, just a simple gathering of religious leaders to make a collective statement: hate has no home here. I wasn't sure who would come and was even rebuked by some of the pastors I invited. The divisions between mainline Protestant pastors and evangelical pastors in Hastings were deep and often unspoken. There was no formal ministerial alliance in town. Mainline pastors like me tended to gather with other mainliners: Methodists, Lutherans, Episcopalians, while evangelical pastors often stuck to their own networks—if they collaborated at all. We lived in parallel ministry worlds, rarely intersecting despite serving the same zip code.

But that morning, something unexpected happened. Standing near the steps was a man with a warm smile and a quiet, confident presence. He introduced himself simply: "I'm John. I pastor the Nazarene church." He extended his hand and said, "Thanks for organizing this." That handshake turned out to be the start of one of the most meaningful friendships of my ministry.

John and I were an unlikely pair. He had grown up in the Wesleyan-Holiness tradition of the Church of the Nazarene, a denomination with deep roots in revivalism, altar calls, and a high view of personal sanctification. I had been raised and ordained in the Reformed tradition, steeped in liturgy, theological nuance, and the sovereignty of God. John wore jeans and sneakers most Sundays. I wore a Geneva gown and stole. But as we talked on those steps and later over coffee, I discovered that we shared something more important than our theological differences: we both loved Jesus, we both loved our community, and we both wanted the church to be a force for healing, hope, and unity.

Over the next few months, our friendship grew. We met regularly for lunch or coffee. We talked about preaching and pastoring, about the challenges facing our congregations, about the weariness that often accompanies ministry in a polarized world. We swapped stories and sermon ideas. We shared joys and burdens. We prayed for one another. Somewhere along the way, I began to refer to John as a mentor. He had been serving as a pastor for many more decades than I had, and he had a lot of wisdom to share. At first, he resisted the label. But it was precisely John's humility that made it easy to walk alongside him and learn from him as colleagues and companions on the journey.

John had a phrase he used often, almost like a mantra: "Many congregations, one church." For him, the visible divisions between churches—denominational, theological, racial, and political—were real but not ultimate. He believed deeply in the unity of the Body of Christ, and he lived that out with a gentle persistence that challenged me. He invited me to think bigger about what church unity could look like: not just ecumenical dialogue but shared mission, shared prayer, and even shared preaching.

In the spring of 2018, John approached me with an idea that seemed, at first, utterly foreign to my ministry comfort zone. He and a couple of other evangelical pastors were planning a good old-fashioned tent revival. They had secured a grassy lot in town, rented a massive white tent, and were putting together a weeklong schedule of worship services, music, and preaching. The vision was clear: bring people together across denominational lines, proclaim the gospel, and offer hope in a time of confusion and division. Then came the invitation: "Would you preach one night?"

I paused. Everything in me wanted to say no. I'd never preached at a tent revival. I wasn't even sure I believed in tent revivals. I didn't use the language of "altar calls" or "getting saved." I had no idea how a tent full of evangelicals would respond to a Presbyterian pastor in a clerical collar exegeting Greek verbs. I wasn't sure I was the right person for the job.

But I also trusted John. And more than that, I believed in what he was trying to do: bring the church together, bear witness to Christ, and offer good news to a weary world. So I said yes.

The weeks leading up to the revival were full of prayer, planning, and a bit of panic. I thought carefully about what to say and how to say it. I didn't want to pretend to be someone I wasn't, but I also didn't want to stand behind a pulpit and pick theological fights. I wanted to speak from my heart, to preach the gospel as I understood it, in a way that would build bridges rather than walls.

When the night came, I was more nervous than I had been in years. The tent was filled with people: some from my church, many from other churches, some who probably hadn't set foot in any church in years. The music was loud and joyful, the kind that makes you want to clap, even if you're not sure you're on beat. There was a palpable sense of expectation, the kind I rarely feel in traditional worship spaces.

When it was my turn to preach, I stepped up to the mic and took a deep breath. I started by telling the story of Jesus calming the storm in Mark 4. I talked about fear and faith, about the chaos of our times and the peace Christ offers. I didn't raise my voice or pace the stage. I didn't issue an altar call. I just preached the good news as best I could: that in the midst of the storm, Christ is in the boat with us.

Afterward, something remarkable happened. People came up to me not to argue theology but to thank me. One woman said, "I'd never heard a sermon like that before. But it made me feel … safe." A man from a Baptist church said, "You didn't preach like I expected. But I felt the Spirit in your words." Another person simply said, "We need more of this."

That week changed something in me. It softened me. It reminded me that the Spirit doesn't play favorites with denominations. It showed me that shared trust can lead to shared witness. And it gave me a glimpse of what it might look like for the church to be one, as Jesus prayed it would be.

Our local newspaper, the *Hastings Tribune*, covered the event with warmth and curiosity. The headlines read, "Big Tent Revival in Hastings a Community Event" and "Gospel Event Promotes Unity Between Churches." Reporters captured the spirit of the gathering, not just the style or the spectacle but the sincere effort to bridge divides and bear collective witness to Christ's love.

One participant, Leslie Mohling from neighboring Glenvil, said to the Tribune, "It's people worshipping Christ, and they're not worshipping under a church name, they're coming together to worship the body of Christ."[1] That summed it up perfectly. No one was trying to steal sheep from another flock. No one was pushing a particular brand of Christianity. It was about lifting up Jesus and trusting that if we did, the Spirit would draw people in.

After the revival, John and I kept meeting. Our friendship deepened. We spoke together on community panels. We prayed together at vigils. Eventually, we helped convene a new kind of ministerial alliance: not an institutional body with bylaws and dues but a relational network of pastors who cared about one another, who could pray together, and who could show up for one another when it mattered.

This chapter of my ministry reminded me of a core truth: unity doesn't require uniformity. We don't have to agree on every point of doctrine or liturgical style to be the church together. What we need is humility, courage, and a willingness to step outside our comfort zones. We need friendships like the one I have with John: friendships rooted in trust, sustained by prayer, and animated by a shared love for Christ and neighbor.

We still don't agree on everything. John and I probably vote differently, interpret Scripture differently, and preach differently. But that doesn't

1. Jon Huthmacher, "Gospel Event Promotes Unity Between Churches," *Hastings Tribune* (Jun 7, 2018), https://www.hastingstribune.com/news/gospel-event-promotes-unity-between-churches/article_f423f8ce-6a5d-11e8-93f9-dbf6a850e3bf.html.

define or divide us. What unites us is far greater: a desire to be faithful pastors, to serve our city, and to follow Jesus wherever he leads, even if it's into a tent on a hot summer night.

One of the most moving moments of that revival week came not during a sermon but during a prayer. It was a simple, spontaneous prayer offered by a teenage girl who had been helping with setup all week. She stood up during the open prayer time and said, "God, I didn't know churches could work together like this. It gives me hope." It gives me hope, too.

In a red state, in a purple church, in a divided world, we need more of these moments: moments where we come together not despite our differences but because of our shared calling. We need more tents. More courage. More friendships. We may be many congregations. But we are, by God's grace, one church.

Discussion Questions:

1. Crossing Theological Boundaries: In what ways did this chapter model how to build friendships across theological or denominational lines? What qualities or practices made our relationship possible? How might you practice similar bridge-building in your own community?
2. Comfort Zones and Courage: I describe preaching at the tent revival as "way out of my comfort zone." When have you stepped out of your own comfort zone for the sake of unity or community? What did you learn from the experience?
3. Unity Without Uniformity: This chapter emphasizes the idea that "unity doesn't require uniformity." What does this mean to you? How can churches remain true to their theological convictions while also collaborating across divides?
4. Shared Public Witness: The initial connection between me and John began with a shared stand against racism. How can shared public witness to justice and compassion serve as a foundation for deeper relationships among diverse churches?
5. Hope for the Next Generation: A teenager at the revival said, "I didn't know churches could work together like this. It gives me hope." What would it take for the next generation to regularly witness this kind of unity? What role can you or your church play in making that vision a reality?

Reflection on John 17:20–23 and Chapter 10

In John 17, Jesus prays for his disciples, and not just for them but for all who would come to believe through their witness. That prayer stretches across the centuries, reaching all the way to us. At its heart is a simple but profound longing: "that they may all be one." Jesus imagines a unity that mirrors the very life of the Trinity: "As you, Father, are in me and I am in you, may they also be in us." This is not unity for unity's sake, nor is it a demand for uniformity. It is a unity rooted in love, a unity that reflects God's own character, a unity that is meant to be visible "so that the world may believe."

The irony is that the church has often failed to embody that prayer. Across denominations, traditions, and even within congregations, we are quick to let differences divide us. Yet Jesus' prayer is not simply wishful thinking. It is a promise: the same glory that the Father gave to the Son, the Son has given to us, "so that they may be one." Unity is not something we create; it is something we receive as a gift of grace and something we are called to live into by the Spirit's power.

That truth came alive for me in Hastings in 2018. When I stood on the steps of City Hall after racist flyers were posted around town, I did not expect to find a new friend. I especially did not expect that friend to be a Nazarene pastor named John, someone whose theological language, worship style, and denominational background were so different from mine. But in that handshake and the friendship that followed, I caught a glimpse of Jesus' prayer being answered.

Our unity did not mean erasing our differences. I remained a Presbyterian with a love for liturgy and careful theology. John remained an evangelical Nazarene with a love for revival and holiness. But we discovered that unity is possible when we meet at the foot of the cross, when we share a love for Christ and a love for our community. When John invited me to preach at the tent revival, it stretched me beyond my comfort zone, but it also opened my eyes to the Spirit's work in unexpected places.

Jesus prayed that the world would see our unity and know the love of God. On that summer night, under a big white tent in Hastings, I saw it happen. People from different churches, different traditions, different walks of life gathered to hear the gospel. A teenage girl put it best: "I didn't know churches could work together like this. It gives me hope."

That is the kind of unity Jesus prayed for: not uniformity but a oneness rooted in God's love and visible in our witness. When we dare to step outside our silos, when we risk friendship across dividing lines, when we choose to lift up Jesus together rather than protect our turf, the world catches a glimpse of God's glory. And in a divided world, there is no more powerful testimony than that.

Chapter 11

Haircuts and Hugs

Offering Dignity and Care

Above all, maintain constant love for one another, for love covers a multitude of sins. Be hospitable to one another without complaining. Like good stewards of the manifold grace of God, serve one another with whatever gift each of you has received. Whoever speaks must do so as one speaking the very words of God; whoever serves must do so with the strength that God supplies, so that God may be glorified in all things through Jesus Christ. To him belong the glory and the power for ever and ever. Amen.

—1 Pet 4:8–11 (NRSV)

It started with a conversation: one of those unplanned but Spirit-led moments that happen when you take the time to listen. I had stopped by the local Salvation Army one August afternoon, just days before the start of a new school year. They were getting ready for their annual back-to-school backpack giveaway, an event that provides hundreds of local children with the basic supplies they need to start school: pencils, notebooks, glue sticks, folders, crayons. The community rallies every year to fill these backpacks, and the Salvation Army faithfully coordinates the distribution.

I was talking with the pastor who leads the Salvation Army ministry here in Hastings. We were standing in the hallway surrounded by bins of markers and packs of loose-leaf paper when I asked him, "What else do you need? How can our church help?" He looked up from the inventory list and smiled. "You know, we usually have enough school supplies. People are really generous with that. But I always wonder if there's something else we could offer these families. Something that makes them feel seen." That word stuck with me: "seen."

Later that week, during our mission committee meeting at First Presbyterian Church of Hastings, I shared that story. I mentioned that I knew a few members of our congregation who had worked as hairdressers. "What if we offered free haircuts?" I asked. "Nothing fancy—just a way to help kids start the school year feeling clean, confident, and cared for."

There was a moment of silence. It wasn't skepticism—it was surprise. Our church had done a lot of mission work over the years: food drives, disaster relief, mission trips, coat collections. But this idea was different. It wasn't about sending money or collecting goods. It was about opening our doors during the week, welcoming people we didn't know into our building, and offering something deeply personal. One committee member leaned in. "You mean, like, set up salon chairs in Fellowship Hall?" "Exactly," I said. "We could even offer dinner for families waiting their turn."

There was some logistical chatter: Do we have enough hairdressers? Do we need a sign-up sheet? What about liability? By the end of the meeting, we had decided to do it. We would offer free haircuts to any student who showed up with a backpack from the Salvation Army event. No questions asked. No forms to fill out. Just come, sit down, get a haircut, and be loved.

The first day of the haircut event, our Fellowship Hall looked completely different than it did on Sundays. Instead of coffee hour tables and Sunday school crafts, there were mirrors propped up on tables, extension cords running to clippers and blow dryers, capes and combs and curls. Sandwich platters were stacked in the corner, and folding chairs lined the walls where families could wait their turn. And people came.

Some came shyly, uncertain whether they belonged in a space that looked so churchy. Some came with nervous energy, kids bouncing, parents weary. Some spoke no English. Some had clearly been through hard seasons: housing insecurity, job loss, illness. And yet, all were greeted with smiles, kind words, and the gentle reassurance that they were welcome.

Our hairdressers were the real heroes. They showed up with their kits in hand, hearts open, ready to give whatever they could. I remember watching as one of our stylists, Nancy, gently brushed a little girl's bangs aside and asked her how she wanted her hair done for the first day of school. "Like Elsa from Frozen," the girl said. "Elsa it is," Nancy smiled.

Another stylist, a longtime member of the congregation named Joan, carefully clipped a boy's hair while he told her all about his favorite superhero. She nodded as he talked, never missing a beat, and when she turned the chair around for him to see himself in the mirror, he grinned from ear to ear. There was something holy happening in those chairs. You could feel it in the quiet attentiveness of the stylists, in the way the kids sat up straighter when they saw their reflection, in the sandwiches and juice boxes passed out with kindness. These weren't just haircuts. They were acts of dignity. Blessings in disguise. And then there were the hugs.

At first, I thought it might be a fluke. But after each haircut, it kept happening. Children would hug the hairdressers. Parents would tear up. Stylists, in turn, would kneel down to give a warm embrace or place a gentle hand on a shoulder. There was something so human about it, so unguarded, that it caught me off guard. That's when I realized that hugs were part of the ministry, too.

One moment that has stayed with me came near the end of the day. A young mother came in with two children. She didn't speak English, and she looked nervous, unsure. I was able to speak Spanish, so I approached her and began speaking. The woman relaxed a little.

We got her kids into chairs, and our hairdressers went to work with care and warmth, using gestures and smiles to bridge the language gap. Afterward, the woman pointed to her own hair and raised her eyebrows. It took a moment to understand, but then Nancy nodded and waved her toward a chair. She didn't have to—she'd already cut hair all afternoon—but she did. She brushed the woman's hair, trimmed the ends, and gave her a simple, beautiful style. When she was done, the mother stood, tears in her eyes. She gave Nancy the kind of hug that said more than words ever could. It was a thank you, a blessing, a prayer all in one. I watched the whole thing and thought, *This is what church is supposed to be.*

It was only after the event that I began reflecting more deeply on what had happened. On the surface, it was a simple gesture: haircuts and sandwiches. But something far more profound had taken place. We had become a vessel of grace, a community of embrace. We had crossed lines—racial lines, linguistic lines, class lines, political lines—and found ourselves standing on common ground.

You see, the volunteers who showed up to cut hair, coordinate, and serve meals that day weren't all politically aligned. In fact, some of them were on opposite ends of the political spectrum. I've seen their yard signs. I've read their Facebook posts. But that day, it didn't matter. That day, they were united by something bigger: the belief that every child deserves the dignity of a back-to-school haircut, that every parent deserves a moment of kindness, that every stranger deserves to be welcomed.

We didn't hold a theological debate about who belonged or what they believed. We didn't ask anyone to prove their citizenship or recite a creed. We just opened the doors and offered what we had. Jesus had something to say about that. In Matt 25, he tells the parable of the sheep and the goats, describing a final judgment based not on belief statements but on acts of compassion: feeding the hungry, clothing the naked, welcoming the stranger. "Just as you did it to one of the least of these," he says, "you did it to me." I've always preached that passage as a call to justice. But that day, it became incarnate. It became haircuts and hugs.

There's something quietly radical about showing hospitality in a divided world. When polarization dominates headlines and fear keeps people isolated, a shared sandwich or a haircut can feel like a small act of rebellion. It pushes back against the narrative that says we must fear the other, that difference is dangerous, that the church is only for the already converted.

That week, the gospel echoed through the hum of clippers and the laughter of children. And our congregation felt it. In the weeks that followed, I heard story after story from our members about what the event had meant to them. One volunteer told me, "I used to think mission was something we did *for* people. Now I think it's something we do *with* people." Another said, "That day, I saw Jesus—in a little boy's eyes, in a mom's hug, in a hairdresser's hands."

In an age of polarization, the church must reclaim the power of the ordinary. We don't always need a statement or a strategy. Sometimes we just need scissors and sandwiches. Sometimes we just need to see people not as political enemies or theological problems but as neighbors, as children of God.

That's what happened that day. People were seen. Dignity was restored. A little girl walked out of Fellowship Hall feeling like Elsa. A mom walked out with a tear-streaked smile. And a group of Presbyterians—many of whom would disagree on almost every ballot initiative—stood together in a shared expression of love. Haircuts and hugs. That's what we had to give. And by God's grace, it was more than enough.

Discussion Questions:

1. Acts of Dignity and Hospitality: Why do you think something as simple as a haircut can be such a powerful act of dignity and hospitality? How might the church rediscover its calling to offer care in ordinary, relational ways?
2. Unity in Service Despite Division: Volunteers from across the political and theological spectrum came together to serve. What made this possible? How can your church or community foster that kind of unity?
3. Seeing and Being Seen: We reflected that families didn't just receive services: they were seen. Why is it important to not only meet needs but to acknowledge the humanity of others? How do we offer "sacred visibility" to our neighbors?
4. Church Beyond Sunday: How does this story challenge traditional notions of what "church" looks like? What opportunities exist for your church to open its doors and become a space of grace during the week?
5. The Ministry of Presence and Touch: The hugs after the haircuts became a form of ministry in themselves. In an increasingly disconnected world, what does this teach us about the power of presence, physical touch, and embodied compassion?

Reflection on 1 Pet 4:8–11 and Chapter 11

The day our fellowship hall was turned into a pop-up salon, I saw this Scripture come alive. There were no grand speeches, no theological debates, no carefully crafted mission statements. Just scissors, clippers, sandwiches, and a community gathered to share what they had. And yet, in those ordinary offerings, the manifold grace of God was on full display.

Peter's call to "maintain constant love" reminds us that the heart of Christian life is not perfection but persistence. Love doesn't erase our differences or solve every disagreement, but it covers them. On haircut day, people who likely would have argued on Facebook about politics or policy instead stood side by side, serving sandwiches, trimming bangs, and laughing with children. Love covered a multitude of divisions, not by ignoring them but by making them seem small compared to the task at hand.

"Be hospitable to one another without complaining," Peter writes. Hospitality is not glamorous work. It can be exhausting, messy, and inconvenient. But that day, the hospitality flowed without complaint—hairdressers on their feet for hours, volunteers sweeping floors, translators bridging language barriers. Each one serving with the gift they had received: a steady hand with scissors, a smile that reassured a nervous child, a pot of coffee for weary parents, a few words of Spanish to help someone feel at home.

Peter goes on: "Whoever serves must do so with the strength that God supplies, so that God may be glorified." This is what made the day holy. The hugs, the tears, the joy were not about us or what we had achieved. They were about God's glory made visible in the love of neighbor. A simple haircut became a sacrament of grace. A hug became a prayer. Hospitality became worship.

The manifold grace of God is just that: manifold. It takes many forms—bread broken at a communion table, words spoken from a pulpit but also scissors in a fellowship hall and sandwiches passed across a table. Each act, when offered in love, becomes a channel of God's grace.

Paul concludes the passage, "To God belong the glory and the power forever and ever. Amen."

Chapter 12

The Church and the US–Mexico Border

As they came near the village to which they were going, he walked ahead as if he were going on. But they urged him strongly, saying, "Stay with us, because it is almost evening and the day is now nearly over." So he went in to stay with them. When he was at the table with them, he took bread, blessed and broke it, and gave it to them. Then their eyes were opened, and they recognized him …

—Luke 24:28–31 (NRSV)

First Presbyterian Church of Hastings has been connected to the US-Mexico border for more than twenty years, long before I arrived here as their senior pastor. The connection started with Susie Frerichs, a Hastings College alum who went to seminary and began serving as a Presbyterian mission worker on the border in Eagle Pass/Piedras Negras in the early 2000s. Once she was working there, groups from Hastings College and First Presbyterian Church of Hastings went down to visit her and learn about what was happening on the border. This was before the border had become as politicized. This relationship with the border went on for a number of years but declined in 2012 when Susie moved into the interior of Mexico.

It was reengaged by the church in 2015, and a delegation visited the border in 2016, this time to the border towns of Douglas/Agua Prieta and the Presbyterian border ministry Frontera de Cristo. At their suggestion, we hosted visitors from the border in Nebraska in 2017 during my first year as a pastor here, and then I helped lead a delegation that returned to the border in 2018, weeks before the mid-term election cycle when the phrase "caravan of immigrants" was being used to try to stoke voter turnout.

The trip in 2018 was a turning point. It was the first time many in our congregation had seen the border wall up close, heard the stories of asylum seekers, and worshiped in Spanish. We met mothers who had walked hundreds of miles with their children. We heard from Border Patrol agents and humanitarian workers. We prayed in two languages.

After that trip, I wrote an article titled "Fearless Generosity and Radical Hospitality" for the Presbyterian Outlook. In it, I reflected on how our group was welcomed with such grace and warmth by people who had so little materially but so much spiritually. I quoted Heb 13:2: "Do not neglect to show hospitality to strangers, for by doing that some have entertained angels without knowing it." We were recipients of radical hospitality, and we wanted to bring those stories and that spirit of hospitality back to our hometown in Nebraska. We had already been doing the Spanish classes and hosting the Mexican folkloric dance troupe at our church, but our congregation was inspired to do more.

We scheduled another trip for our sisters and brothers from the border to come visit us in Nebraska in 2019, to continue to demystify the border and the issues associated with it while allowing our church members to have deep and meaningful interactions with people who live on the border. We had fallen into a pattern of taking a trip to the border one year and then hosting visitors from the border the next year, and our congregation was being transformed in the process as we began to see the stories of the border through the lens of our faith.

COVID disrupted our cycle of trips but didn't dampen our spirit for border ministry. We stayed in touch with the team at Frontera de Cristo and sent donations to help them manage COVID issues in the migrant shelters. Once the travel restrictions were lifted, we brought a delegation from the border to Nebraska in 2023. During that visit, an audacious invitation was extended to us by Mark Adams, the Presbyterian mission co-worker and US coordinator of Frontera de Cristo. Would we consider bringing our church choir to the border in 2024 to help celebrate the 40th anniversary of Frontera de Cristo, which would be marked in October?

I knew that this would be weeks before the 2024 presidential election and that border issues and immigration would be a key issue in the election. After consulting our mission committee and the leadership committee of the church, we accepted the invitation and began planning. It was part pilgrimage, part protest, part partnership. We went not only to serve but to listen, to learn, and to be transformed.

The Sunday after we returned from the 2024 Music and Mission trip to the US-Mexico border, I stood in the pulpit of First Presbyterian Church of Hastings and tried to put words to the experience. Our choir had sung in English and Spanish. We prayed and worshiped together. We had stood in the literal shadow of the border wall, held hands with Mexican pastors and church members, and broken bread together in communion. Twenty pilgrims, including four Hastings College students and two community members who participated in our music programs, made the journey. We spanned four generations, from 18 to 80 years old. We carried our sheet music and open hearts.

We performed concerts on both sides of the border, blending traditional hymns with choral pieces and justice-themed music. We shared meals with others, visited community projects, and toured a coffee-roasting cooperative that employs migrants and supports fair trade. At Café Justo, we learned about how economic insecurity is one of the driving forces of migration. We saw how offering just wages and stable employment could reduce the need for people to flee. This was theology with legs, gospel ethics roasted into each pound of coffee. And now we were back in Nebraska, changed.

I looked out at the congregation and said, "When you stand at the border, it's no longer just an abstract issue or a talking point. It's people. It's children and grandparents, students and pastors. It's laughter and tears. It's music that rises above walls."

We had just spent five days on the border, but our perspectives and hearts were forever changed. This trip, timed with the election cycle, felt different. Back home, a member of our church asked me, "Why do we keep going back to the border? Haven't we done enough?" I paused then said, "Because the border keeps coming back to us." What I meant is that border issues like immigration, asylum, xenophobia, and hospitality aren't just about geography; they're about theology. They're about how we treat the stranger, how we see the image of God in every person, and how we live out the gospel in a divided world. These aren't someone else's problems. They are ours.

When we talk about the border, it's tempting to fall into binary thinking: legal vs. illegal, citizen vs. alien, us vs. them. But our trips have taught us that real life, and real faith, is more complex. It's about relationships. It's about hearing stories that disrupt our assumptions. It's about seeing Jesus in the faces of migrants, mission workers, and one another.

I remember a young man named Luis who had been deported from the US after living there since childhood. He spoke perfect English and told us he felt like a foreigner in both countries. "I don't belong anywhere," he said. A college student from our group sat next to him and said, "You belong here. Right now, you're with us."

I also remember María, a woman who works in the Migrant Resource Center for recently returned migrants who have been deported. She told us how her faith sustains her. "Jesus was a migrant," she said. "He fled violence as a child. He had no place to lay his head. So when I welcome others, I welcome him." At the Migrant Resource Center, just steps from the border crossing, migrants who had been deported or who were waiting in limbo received water, food, basic hygiene supplies and compassion. This kind of perspective changes you. It makes you question simplistic narratives and partisan talking points. It makes you wrestle with Scripture, with privilege, and with the meaning of justice. It sends you home with a holy discomfort, that's why we go. We don't go to fix things; we go to be in relationship. We don't go to serve; we go to be in solidarity, to learn and grow together, and to be reminded of our shared humanity. We go because the gospel calls us to go to the margins, to the walls, to the hard places where Jesus is already present.

In one of our evening devotionals, someone said, "The wall is built to separate, but music brings us together." That became something of a refrain for us. At a concert we held on the Mexican side of the border in an amphitheater in the town square of Agua Prieta, a woman came up to our choir and said, "You sang like angels. We haven't heard this kind of music here before." Another evening, we stood in the lobby of the historic Gadsen Hotel in Douglas and sang, "For everyone born, a place at the table, for everyone born, clean water and bread. A shelter a space, a safe place for growing. For everyone born, a star overhead. And God will delight when we are creators of justice, joy, compassion, and peace." Tears flowed freely, not as a performance but as prayer.

One of the key theological themes that emerged from our trip was the idea of *acompañamiento*: accompaniment. This is not the same as leadership or charity. It is about walking with. It is the Emmaus Road model of mission: traveling alongside others, breaking bread, sharing stories, and encountering Christ in the midst. We didn't go to the border to solve anything. We went to bear witness, to listen deeply, to humanize what has been politicized, and to find Christ in unexpected places.

When we returned to Hastings, we brought back more than photos and memories. We brought back stories, songs, and a renewed sense of call. Our congregation listened attentively as pilgrims shared in worship and adult education forums. Some confessed that they'd never thought much about immigration before. Others said they'd changed their minds about what it means to be a neighbor. Still others said they were proud that our church was willing to go to the margins, both geographically and spiritually.

The US-Mexico border is not just a line on a map. It's a mirror, showing us who we are and who we might become. And if we let it, it can be a place of grace, a place where music and mission meet, a place where strangers become neighbors, a place where, even through steel slats and political barriers, the body of Christ is broken and shared. It is a place where we wrestle and where we are blessed.

In a deeply polarized time, and in a deeply red state, our church's border ministry has become a surprising source of unity rather than division. While our congregation includes people with a wide range of political views, we've found common ground not in debating immigration policy but in responding to the gospel's call to compassion, presence, and partnership. When we center our shared faith rather than our partisan identities, we discover that things like hospitality, dignity, and love of neighbor aren't red or blue issues: they're Christian commitments. And in walking alongside those at the margins, we've found ourselves walking closer together as a church, reclaiming our purple identity, not by avoiding hard issues but by engaging them with courage, humility, and hope.

Discussion Questions:

1. How have your views on immigration and the US-Mexico border been shaped by personal experiences, media, or political discourse? How does this chapter challenge or complicate those perspectives?
2. The chapter emphasizes "radical hospitality" and "holy discomfort." What do those phrases mean to you in the context of Christian faith? Where in your life have you encountered that tension between comfort and calling?
3. "We don't go to fix things; we go to be in relationship." How does this understanding of mission differ from more traditional models of service or charity? How might it change the way your congregation approaches mission work?
4. In what ways is the border — or the issues symbolized by it — "coming back to us" in our own communities? What would it mean to respond theologically rather than politically?
5. The chapter ends by describing the border as a mirror and a place of grace. What do you think it is revealing about us as individuals, as churches, and as a nation? Where do you see opportunities for transformation and hope?

Reflection on Luke 24:28–31 and Chapter 12

On the Emmaus Road, the disciples were disoriented, overwhelmed by grief, and unsure of how to make sense of the events swirling around them. A stranger drew near and walked with them, listening to their sorrow, reframing their story, and breaking bread at their table. In that moment of hospitality and companionship, their eyes were opened, and they recognized Christ in their midst.

That story has become a model for our border ministry at First Presbyterian Church of Hastings. When we travel to the US-Mexico border, we don't go as experts or problem-solvers. We go as companions. We walk the road alongside migrants, pastors, mission workers, and families whose lives are shaped by the border. We listen to their stories of loss, hope, resilience, and faith. We break bread together, sometimes literally at communion, sometimes in the form of tamales in a church fellowship hall or coffee from

Café Justo roasted with dignity and justice in every bean. And in those moments, our eyes are opened.

We begin to recognize Christ in the faces of mothers carrying children across deserts, in the weary eyes of deported sons and daughters, in the strong voices of those who sing hymns on both sides of the wall. The wall is built to divide, but like the disciples on the Emmaus Road, we discover that Jesus draws near in places of division, walking with us, sharing our sorrows, and revealing God's presence in the breaking of bread.

One of our pilgrims said, "We don't go to fix anything; we go to walk with." That is the heart of *acompañamiento*, the theology of accompaniment. Just as Christ accompanied those disciples on the road, so too are we called to accompany our neighbors at the margins. Not rushing ahead, not hanging back, but walking alongside.

And like the disciples, we return home changed. The border is no longer abstract or distant; it is personal, relational, and theological. Our eyes have been opened, and we can no longer see migrants as headlines or statistics. We see them as neighbors, as family, as bearers of Christ's presence.

The Emmaus story ends with the disciples running back to Jerusalem to share what they had seen. Our border ministry has a similar rhythm. We return to Hastings with stories and songs, inviting our congregation to see what we have seen, to hear what we have heard, and to join us in living out the gospel call to love the stranger and break bread together as one body.

In a divided world, the Emmaus Road reminds us that Christ is still showing up in the walking, the listening, the eating, and the sharing. At the border, in Nebraska, wherever hospitality is offered and bread is broken, our eyes are opened again and we recognize him.

Chapter 13

Let's Just Have Supper

Table Fellowship as Grace

When they had gone ashore, they saw a charcoal fire there, with fish on it, and bread. Jesus said to them, "Bring some of the fish that you have just caught." So Simon Peter went aboard and hauled the net ashore, full of large fish, a hundred and fifty-three of them; and though there were so many, the net was not torn. Jesus said to them, "Come and have breakfast." Now none of the disciples dared to ask him, "Who are you?" because they knew it was the Lord. Jesus came and took the bread and gave it to them, and did the same with the fish.

—John 21:9–13 (NRSV)

In the fall of 2018, as political divisions in the country deepened and the fabric of civic discourse seemed to fray further each day, my wife, Jessica, had an idea. What if we simply sat down and had supper together? What if, instead of trying to fix each other's politics or theology, we simply shared a meal, passed the bread, and offered grace—not just in the blessing but in the way we listened and laughed and lingered? Thus began what came to be known as the Sunday Night Supper Series.

We didn't start with an agenda beyond sharing food. We opened the invitation up to the whole church, which included people from all ends of the political and theological spectrum. Jessica would make the main course, a white chicken chili, and invite others to bring sides, salads, and desserts. This was one of our first introductions to Midwest "salads." People would arrive with something that didn't include any green vegetables and often incorporated Jello, and we weren't sure if it was a side, a salad, or a dessert. Usually it was called a "salad," and we would put it out to be enjoyed with the main courses. If people came over with their kids, the children would go out and play in the backyard if it wasn't too cold or windy. The adults would stand in the kitchen and talk. We talked about Nebraska Cornhuskers football (or volleyball), the weather, and our kids or grandkids. Occasionally, we ventured into more delicate territory. But the supper table, unlike the internet or the town hall, created a buffer of grace. The smell of fresh-baked cornbread and chili in the crockpot softened our edges.

We kept it going for half the year, hosting these gatherings a few times a month. As we did this, something sacred began to unfold: a re-weaving of community threads that had been frayed by campaign signs and Facebook posts. We learned that the person who voted differently also makes a mean apple pie and that someone with a radically different theological view had lost a spouse and could cry and laugh just like the rest of us.

What we practiced was table fellowship. In the early church, breaking bread together was one of the most radical acts of community. Jesus did this over and over: eating with tax collectors, prostitutes, Pharisees, and friends. The table was a place where hierarchies were broken down. In Luke's Gospel, the resurrected Christ is recognized not in a sermon or a miracle but in the breaking of the bread with the two disciples on the road to Emmaus. At the table, something is revealed.

One Sunday, someone asked if we could begin the meal with a song. Someone else offered a prayer. Another night, one of the kids asked if we could help them with their homework. These weren't part of the plan, but neither was Pentecost, and that turned out okay. The Spirit showed up. At the table.

This story of shared meals reminds me of a beautiful song written by Korby Lenker and Nora Jane Struthers called "Let's Just Have Supper." A verse and the chorus of the song read:

> Scrollin' through my feed's / Like chasin' down a ghost
> It's not a conversation / It's just comments on a post
> I guess we got a mess / There ain't no easy fix

> But supper's on and it's almost done / Why don't you come on by round six?
> Everybody needs to eat
>
> Let's just have supper / Here, pull up a chair
> It's hard to feel so far away / Sitting with you here
> Cornbread's in the oven / Chicken's on the stove
> Let's just have supper / Before the beans get cold

The song is deceptively simple, but its message is profound. In a world where we often lead with critique, where conversation quickly becomes confrontation, what would it mean to check our arguments, our rebuttals, our righteous certainties at the door? What if we just had supper?

Over the course of those months, I began to see transformation. Not everyone changed their views. But they changed how they saw one another. The staunch conservative elder and the progressive college professor who barely spoke in church leadership council meetings now swapped recipes. A young parent who had been suspicious of the older generation started a babysitting swap with an empty-nester. One man told me, "You know, I used to think she was nuts. But now I see she's just passionate and kind."

The supper table didn't solve everything. There were still tensions. People still disagreed. But the disagreements felt different after you had passed someone the potatoes. It's hard to dehumanize someone who brought you peach cobbler.

Jesus was accused of many things—blasphemy, sedition, and one rather telling accusation: "This man eats with sinners." As if that were the worst thing he did. But maybe it was the best. Eating with people who weren't supposed to be at the same table was Jesus's modus operandi. And it still is.

In a politically purple church, table fellowship becomes not just a quaint tradition but a radical act. It's a countercultural witness that says we belong to one another, even when we disagree. We're called not only to pass the peace in worship but to pass the peas in fellowship. Not to convince each other of our own righteousness but to confess our common humanity.

One particularly memorable night, a church member brought a friend who had never been to a church gathering before. She didn't know the creeds or the liturgy. But halfway through the meal, she turned to me and said, "Is this what you people mean when you talk about communion?" I laughed and said, "Something like that." And then I paused. Because it was exactly that.

There was no chalice or platter, no formal liturgy. But there was bread. There was gratitude. There was presence. And in that presence, something holy.

Another evening, just before Advent, someone brought tamales, and someone else brought Snickers salad, and somehow it worked. These weren't just foods. They were memories, stories, and invitations. The diversity of dishes mirrored the diversity of stories around the table, and the Spirit wove it all together into a feast of reconciliation.

In those moments, I found myself thinking of Jesus' post-resurrection meals. He didn't deliver great lectures. He grilled fish. He offered bread. He joined the disciples in their everyday hungers. The divine was revealed not in thunder or fire but in flavor, fellowship, and full bellies.

Years later, church members still reference those suppers. They say things like, "Remember when Roger brought that spicy dish that made us all sweat?" Or "Remember when all that people brought were desserts?" These aren't just stories. They are sacraments of memory, moments when the church was not just a building or a program but a gathered people practicing grace.

Since then, we've tried to bring that spirit of table fellowship into other aspects of church life. Potlucks, coffee hours, shared meals with our mission partners. We've invited our neighbors, hosted combined meals and worship services with other churches, and sat at tables where we didn't know everyone's name. Because if Christ is known in the breaking of the bread, then every table has the potential to be a sacred space.

I don't know what the next election cycle will bring. I don't know what theological debates will rise to the surface in the wider church. But I do know this: at First Presbyterian Church of Hastings, Nebraska, we'll keep setting the table. We'll keep making chili. We'll keep inviting people to come hungry and leave filled—not just with food but with hope. And maybe, just maybe, with a little more understanding of the neighbor across the table. Let's just have supper.

Discussion Questions:

1. What are some memories you have of meals that brought people together across lines of difference?
2. How does table fellowship reflect the ministry of Jesus and the early church?

3. What makes sharing a meal such a powerful tool for reconciliation and relationship-building?
4. How might your congregation or community create spaces for this kind of shared table fellowship?
5. In what ways can the act of eating together become a form of communion in our daily lives?

Reflection on John 21:9–13 and Chapter 13

After the confusion of crucifixion and the wonder of resurrection, the disciples returned to what was familiar: fishing. When they came ashore, weary from their labor, Jesus was waiting with a charcoal fire, bread, and fish already prepared. He didn't give them a lecture, a strategy, or a sermon. He gave them breakfast. Around the fire, with food in hand, their faith was rekindled, their hope restored, and their fellowship renewed.

That same spirit was alive in our Sunday Night Supper Series. In a season of deep polarization, when campaign signs lined streets and Facebook posts made neighbors strangers, we set a table. There was no agenda beyond food and fellowship. Chili simmered, cornbread baked, and someone inevitably brought a Midwestern "salad" that defied culinary categories. Children played in the yard, adults gathered in the kitchen, and the Spirit found its way into laughter, stories, and even the silence.

Like the disciples on the shore, we discovered that meals open our eyes to Christ's presence in surprising ways. A conservative elder and a progressive professor shared recipes. A young parent found unexpected support from an older member. Disagreements remained, but they softened after you had passed the potatoes.

In John's Gospel, the risen Christ makes himself known not through spectacle but through supper. Bread in hand, fish on the fire, love embodied in the most ordinary of acts. That is the same love that showed up in our suppers. One guest, unfamiliar with church, asked if this was what Christians mean by communion. She was right. It was communion—food and fellowship turned sacramental by presence, gratitude, and love.

The table did not erase our differences, but it transformed how we saw one another. Just as the disciples knew it was the Lord when he broke bread, we too came to recognize Christ in our neighbors, even those who saw the world differently.

In an age where so much divides us, the call of John 21 still echoes: "Come and have breakfast." Or in our case, "Come and have supper." Because every shared meal has the potential to be holy ground, every table a place where Christ is revealed in bread, laughter, and the love that binds us together.

Chapter 14

"In God We Trust" Signs

Trusting God, Trusting Each Other

With what shall I come before the Lord, and bow myself before God on high?
Shall I come before him with burnt-offerings, with calves a year old?
Will the Lord be pleased with thousands of rams, with tens of thousands of rivers of oil?
Shall I give my firstborn for my transgression, the fruit of my body for the sin of my soul?
He has told you, O mortal, what is good; and what does the Lord require of you
but to do justice, and to love kindness, and to walk humbly with your God?

—*Mic 6:6–8 (NRSV)*

In October 2018, a member of my congregation who also served on the Adams County Board of Supervisors knocked on my office door with what he thought would be a straightforward request. He had been asked to support a proposal to place a large sign reading "In God We Trust" on the courthouse in downtown Hastings. As a Christian pastor, he assumed I would be eager to help him craft remarks in favor of the initiative.

What he received instead was not a lecture or a rebuke but a conversation. I told him that while I do, indeed, trust in God, and while that trust grounds my entire life and calling, I wasn't convinced that fastening those words to a government building was the best way to bear witness to that trust. My concern was not rooted in hostility toward faith but rather in a desire to protect it: protecting both the freedom to believe and the freedom not to.

Not long after, another member of our church submitted a counter-proposal: if the courthouse was going to display religious messages, why not hang a banner of equal size proclaiming the Eleven Rules of Satan? She wasn't a Satanist; she was making a civic point. Her husband, a veteran and an atheist, had risked his life for freedom, and she asked why he should be confronted with a government-sponsored religious declaration every time he went to pay his property taxes.

In the eyes of many in the community, her protest looked like blasphemy. In reality, it was a plea for fairness. And here's the twist: she and the county supervisor sat in the same pews on Sunday morning.

Suddenly our purple church was face-to-face with the tension between conviction and community.

I found myself sitting with both of them, sometimes separately, sometimes together, listening to their stories, their reasoning, their hopes. The goal wasn't to "win" the argument but to stay at the table. I tried to model what it means to practice civil discourse: listening deeply, affirming the sincerity of each person's faith (or doubt), and acknowledging the genuine fears and hopes on both sides.

In the end, the sign went up. For some, it's still a symbol of pride. For others, it's a reminder that not everyone feels equally represented by their government. But for our church, the more enduring lesson wasn't about the sign on the courthouse. It was about how two people, who saw the world so differently, kept showing up on Sunday and sharing a pew.

Fast forward to 2024. The same phrase, "In God We Trust," was back: this time proposed for every classroom in the Hastings Public Schools. Three members of our church who served on the school board came to me, each asking the same question in slightly different words: How can I oppose this faithfully, as a Christian?

That question revealed the heart of the matter. These weren't people trying to push faith aside; they were people who prayed, read Scripture, and raised their children in the church. Their hesitation wasn't about belief but about compulsion. Together, we reflected on the nature of their witness: that faith shines brightest not when it is required but when it is freely chosen.

We talked about what it means to live in a pluralistic society. Could Christians ask for freedom to worship in countries where they are a minority, while denying that same freedom to non-Christians here at home? Pope Francis once put it this way in *Fratelli Tutti*: "We Christians ask that, in those countries where we are a minority, we be guaranteed freedom, even as we ourselves promote that freedom for non-Christians in places where they are a minority."[1]

When the school board voted, the proposal failed. Not because the board was hostile to religion but because its members, including my three parishioners, understood that religious liberty is strongest when it protects everyone.

These two episodes, one ending with a sign on the courthouse wall, the other with a proposal turned back at the schoolhouse door, helped me see something essential about life in a purple church. The real story isn't the vote tally. It's the way people with deep disagreements stayed in relationship. It's the willingness of church members to wrestle with how to be faithful Christians in a pluralistic society.

At the end of the day, our purple church is full of people who do trust in God. They also trust that God is bigger than our signs and slogans. They trust that the best testimony isn't necessarily etched in stone above a courthouse or pinned to a classroom wall; it's lived out in daily acts of love, kindness, and justice.

That is the gift of being a purple church together in a red state. Not uniformity but the hard, holy work of remaining in community even when our convictions diverge. Not the erasure of difference but the refusal to let difference sever the bonds of fellowship.

In God we do trust. And in God's grace, we keep learning how to trust one another, too.

1. Pope Francis, *Fratelli Tutti* (Vatican: Holy See, Oct 4, 2020), https://www.vatican.va/content/francesco/en/encyclicals/documents/papa-francesco_20201003_enciclica-fratelli-tutti.html.

Discussion Questions:

1. How do we distinguish between personal expressions of faith and public, government-sponsored religious statements?
2. What risks do we run when faith becomes entangled with political or civic authority?
3. In what ways can disagreement over deeply held convictions become an opportunity for deeper relationship rather than division?
4. How does our understanding of religious liberty shape our witness as Christians in a pluralistic society?
5. What does it mean to "trust in God" in ways that transcend signs, slogans, or public declarations?

Reflection on Mic 6:6–8 and Chapter 14

The people of Israel wanted to know what God expected from them. Should they offer sacrifices? Rivers of oil? Even their children? The prophet Micah responded with a resounding no. God is not looking for outward displays of piety or religious slogans carved into stone. God is looking for a way of life marked by justice, kindness, and humility.

This ancient tension between outward signs of devotion and the inward life of faith echoed in Hastings when debates over the phrase "In God We Trust" erupted in our courthouse and schools. For some, the words were an affirmation of faith and heritage. For others, they were a troubling sign of government-sponsored religion that excluded neighbors who did not share the same belief. And in our purple church, those differing perspectives weren't abstract: they sat shoulder-to-shoulder in the same pews.

In those moments, I was reminded of Micah's challenge. What does the Lord require? Not signs on a wall but lives that reflect God's justice and mercy. Not compulsion but conviction. Not slogans but service.

The truth is, signs can inspire or divide, but they cannot substitute for faith lived out in community. The real testimony of our church was not whether we agreed about the courthouse or the classroom but whether we kept showing up together. Whether we could trust that God is bigger than our disagreements. Whether we could practice justice, kindness, and humility, even when we voted differently.

And perhaps that is what a purple church in a red state is called to demonstrate: that the deepest witness of faith is not etched into granite or mandated in classrooms but written on human hearts and lived in daily acts of compassion. In God we do trust, and because of that trust, we strive to walk humbly, love kindly, and do justice together.

Chapter 15

Seeking Relief from Floods and Polarization

But now thus says the Lord, he who created you, O Jacob, he who formed you, O Israel: Do not fear, for I have redeemed you; I have called you by name, you are mine.
When you pass through the waters, I will be with you; and through the rivers, they shall not overwhelm you; when you walk through fire you shall not be burned, and the flame shall not consume you. For I am the Lord your God, the Holy One of Israel, your Savior.

—*Isa 43:1–3 (NRSV)*

In 2019, the Season of Lent—those six weeks leading up to Easter—began the way it often does in the Great Plains: with gray skies, cold winds, and the slow promise of spring still hidden beneath layers of snow and ice. As the church entered that season of repentance, reflection, and preparation, none of us could have predicted how literal the wilderness would become.

In March of that year, a "bomb cyclone" weather event tore through the Midwest, dropping torrential rain on still-frozen ground. The resulting runoff overwhelmed rivers, broke levees, and swallowed towns. Nebraska experienced some of the worst flooding in its recorded history. Entire communities were cut off from the rest of the state, roads and bridges were washed away, and family farms, some in operation for generations, were left submerged or destroyed.

I remember sitting in my office when the phone rang. It was a member of our congregation, Ashley, whose quiet strength had become a comforting presence in my first couple years at First Presbyterian Church. "Pastor," she said, her voice trembling slightly, "have you seen the news from Spencer?"

Spencer, Nebraska, a town of barely four hundred people near the South Dakota border, was where Ashley had grown up. The Spencer Dam had failed, and the resulting flood had swept away homes, livestock, and livelihoods. She paused for a moment and then asked, almost apologetically, "Do you think we could maybe put out a couple of bins in the hallway to collect flood relief supplies for the people up there?"

What happened next was one of those moments in ministry when the Spirit seems to blow through a church like a prairie wind. We didn't just fill a couple of bins. Within a few days, our fellowship hall began to fill with donations. Water bottles, cleaning supplies, work gloves, hygiene kits, baby formula, socks, and boots: the items arrived faster than we could sort them. Our congregation responded with a generosity that stunned even the organizers. People who hadn't come to worship in months showed up with boxes of goods and checks in hand. Our youth group took it upon themselves to pack supplies into boxes and label everything for distribution. Church members shared posts on social media, and suddenly donations were arriving from friends in Lincoln, Kearney, even as far away as Fort Collins, Colorado.

By the end of the week, we had a church van, two pickup trucks, and a trailer loaded to the brim with relief supplies. We drove the caravan four hours to the flood relief center that had been set up at Boyd County Public Schools in Spencer. Our route was circuitous because many bridges and roads had been washed out by the flooding, but we finally arrived. The volunteers there had been working nonstop and looked weary but grateful. As we unloaded the trucks, I watched tears stream down one volunteer's face. "You have no idea how much this means to us," she said.

That might have been the end of it: a successful supply drive and a feel-good story about the generosity of a local church. But something had been stirred in the congregation. People began asking, "What else can we do?"

It started with a small group, mostly members of the mission committee and a few others who weren't afraid to get their hands dirty, who suggested we organize a day trip to do flood relief work. A few weeks later, we loaded up the church van and half a dozen pickup trucks and SUVs and headed to Wood River, a community that had been hit hard by the flooding and was still reeling from the damage. We were assigned to a handful of homes and asked to pull up water-logged flooring, tear out drywall, haul debris, and do whatever the homeowners needed. It was gritty, unglamorous work, but the kind that builds community. A local catering company heard about our trip and donated sandwiches and cookies for the volunteers and the community. In between jobs, we shared those sandwiches and stories with locals who were overwhelmed by the support from strangers.

One homeowner, an elderly man who had lived in his house for more than fifty years, stood in his torn-up living room with tears in his eyes. "I didn't think anyone would come," he said quietly. "I figured everyone had forgotten about us." We told him we hadn't.

That trip sparked something larger. Our mission committee began exploring what more we could do, not just in the immediate aftermath of disaster but in sustained partnership with those who had been affected, especially those who were often left behind in such recoveries.

By the time summer arrived, we had put together a full adult mission trip. This wasn't something our church had done in a few years, and the idea was met with both excitement and logistical anxiety. Where would we go? Who would lead it? What kind of work would we do?

After several conversations and much prayer, we decided to travel to the Pine Ridge Reservation in South Dakota. The reservation had been hit hard by spring flooding as well, and the needs were immense—not just because of the disaster but because of the systemic poverty caused by the relocation of Native Americans to reservations that had already shaped life there. We reached out to local leaders, including Henry Red Cloud, a Lakota elder and renewable energy advocate who had become a key voice in efforts to bring sustainability and dignity to Native communities.

Through Henry's connections and guidance, we planned a week of service focused on flood relief and home repair: clean-up, reconstruction, and partnering with tribal members to address immediate needs. It was important to us that we didn't show up with a savior mentality. We didn't want to be a group of white Christians from Nebraska swooping in to "fix" things. We wanted to listen, to learn, and to serve alongside.

To our surprise and delight, we were joined by a group of men from an evangelical church in Washington state. They had heard about our trip through a mutual connection and asked if they could partner with us. We said yes, and our group grew to include not only Presbyterians and evangelicals but also a few unaffiliated neighbors who were curious and wanted to help.

The team slept in sleeping bags in a community center and ate communal meals prepared by a rotating group of volunteers. Each morning began with prayer and reflection. One of the Washington men said, at the end of the first day, "I didn't expect to be working alongside Presbyterians. Y'all are more open-hearted than I'd been led to believe." We laughed and told him the feeling was mutual. We found common ground not through doctrine but through drywall and shared sweat.

One of the most meaningful days was spent helping an elder named Lorraine, whose home had taken on several inches of water. Her kitchen floor had buckled, and mold was spreading along the baseboards. She welcomed the team with coffee and told us about her grandchildren, who lived with her. As they worked, Lorraine shared stories about her people: about the beauty of the Lakota language and the struggles of reservation life. She didn't sugarcoat anything. "We've been flooded for generations," she said. "Water just makes it visible."

By the end of the week, our team had spent a week sweating and doing flood relief work. But perhaps more importantly, they had been changed. They had listened and learned. They had broken bread with new friends and witnessed a strength that humbled us.

Back home, as the team reported back to the congregation, they reflected on what this trip had meant. It was tempting to talk about "what was accomplished," but they tried to focus instead on what they received. One church member said it best: "This wasn't about doing something for others; it was about being with others. And realizing we're not as different as we think."

Of course, not everyone saw it that way. As images of the Nebraska floods dominated headlines, so did commentary about global climate change, infrastructure decay, and federal disaster spending. The political debates were fierce: some argued that the flooding was proof of the climate crisis and called for urgent action, while others dismissed it as a rare weather anomaly. Online comment sections became battlegrounds. At one point, someone posted an op-ed in the local paper blaming climate activists for politicizing a natural disaster. Others accused the federal government of failing the Midwest.

In our church, we didn't ignore these conversations. We had members on both sides of the climate debate, and some of them expressed their views passionately. But rather than argue about carbon footprints and federal aid, we tried to stay rooted in something simpler and more immediate: the call to love our neighbor.

When someone's home is under water, you don't start by asking their opinion on the Paris Climate Accord. You start by helping them clean out their basement.

In worship during that season, we read from the prophet Isaiah: "When you pass through the waters, I will be with you... when you walk through fire you shall not be burned, and the flame shall not consume you" (Isa 43:2). We reminded each other that our call as Christians is not contingent on political consensus; it's grounded in compassion. It's found in showing up, again and again, when the waters rise.

We also talked about Matt 25, where Jesus tells us that whatever we do for "the least of these," we do for him. That became something of a refrain for us during that year. Not a slogan, not a banner, but a guiding truth. And as we leaned into that truth, our congregation found a renewed sense of purpose. We stopped worrying about whether we would offend someone's politics and started asking instead, "How can we serve?" And while we haven't solved the world's big problems, we've built something more lasting: a witness to what it means to be a community of faith that responds to pain with presence.

We've also built unlikely partnerships. The group from Washington stayed in touch. A few of them have offered to come back for a second trip. One even subscribed to our podcast and started sending me emails with sermon reflections. We don't agree on everything, but we share a love for Jesus and a desire to be his hands and feet in a hurting world. That's enough.

We're not naïve. We know that polarization runs deep and that our country remains divided on issues like environmental policy, disaster response, and the role of the federal government. But at our best, we've discovered that compassion can break through even the hardest divides. That mission doesn't begin with a debate: it begins with a shovel, a mop, and a listening ear.

One morning that fall, after the flooding, I walked into the sanctuary just as the sun was rising. The light was streaming through the stained-glass windows, casting a warm, golden glow over the pews. I thought about

Ashley's phone call. And I thought about how Lent had started in the wilderness but ended with resurrection.

Maybe that's what mission is. Not fixing everything. Not solving all the problems. But entering the wilderness with hope. Sitting with our neighbors in the mud and the mess. Bearing witness to their pain. And reminding them and ourselves that God is with us in the rising waters.

Discussion Questions:

1. The chapter emphasizes responding to human need without getting entangled in political debates. What are the strengths—and potential limitations—of this approach? How can churches discern when to take a prophetic stand and when to simply serve?
2. The adult mission trip to Pine Ridge is described not as an act of charity but as an opportunity for mutual learning and relationship. How does this reframe our understanding of "mission work"? Have you ever had a similar experience of being changed through service?
3. Natural disasters often spark political debates about climate change and government responsibility. How can churches create space for honest dialogue about these issues while staying rooted in their call to love and serve?
4. This chapter includes a partnership with an evangelical church from another state. What do such cross-theological or cross-political partnerships teach us about the body of Christ? What barriers might stand in the way of those relationships, and how can they be overcome?
5. The chapter ends with a reflection on Lent moving toward resurrection. Where have you seen signs of new life emerge from seasons of crisis or destruction—in your community, your church, or your own life?

Reflection on Isa 43:1–3 and Chapter 15

The people of Israel heard these words at a time when their world felt unstable. They were exiles, displaced and discouraged, unsure of whether God had abandoned them. Into that fear, God spoke a word of promise: "Do not fear, for I have redeemed you … when you pass through the waters, I will be with you."

In 2019, when floods swept across Nebraska, those words took on flesh in our community. Waters rose, bridges collapsed, homes were destroyed. Yet in the midst of that chaos, God's promise was visible in the generosity of neighbors, in trucks filled with relief supplies, in volunteers tearing out ruined flooring, and in the prayers and tears shared in waterlogged living rooms.

The floods reminded us that God never promised we wouldn't face the waters. The rivers still rise. The storms still come. But Isaiah insists that even then, we are not alone. God's presence does not remove our suffering: it redeems it, transforming despair into compassion and destruction into community.

Our congregation discovered that mission is not about fixing everything. It is about showing up. It is about answering Ashley's trembling phone call with a fellowship hall full of supplies. It is about driving circuitous routes to Spencer because the bridges are gone, just to say to weary volunteers, "You are not forgotten." It is about joining hands with strangers on the Pine Ridge Reservation, listening to their stories, and realizing that redemption is not just something we preach—it is something we practice, one mop, one prayer, one meal at a time.

Isaiah's promise reminds us that the floods do not have the final word. God does. And God's word is presence, redemption, and hope. When the waters rise again, as they inevitably will in some form, our task is not to debate whose fault it is but to remember who we are: people redeemed, called by name, and sent to bear witness to a God who walks with us through the waters.

Chapter 16

Faith in a Time of Pandemic

Responding to COVID-19 as a Church

God is our refuge and strength, a very present help in trouble. Therefore we will not fear, though the earth should change, though the mountains shake in the heart of the sea; though its waters roar and foam, though the mountains tremble with its tumult... 'Be still, and know that I am God! I am exalted among the nations, I am exalted in the earth.'

—Ps 46:1–3, 10 (NRSV)

In early March of 2020, the word "coronavirus" was still unfamiliar to most of us. It was something happening far away: a health crisis unfolding in distant cities and foreign countries. But within a matter of weeks, the COVID-19 pandemic was no longer an abstract threat. It was here, reshaping every corner of our lives. In Hastings, Nebraska, schools closed, grocery store shelves emptied, and people began to speak in hushed tones about case counts and ventilators.

At First Presbyterian Church, we were in the middle of our Lenten journey, preparing our hearts for Holy Week and Easter. The sanctuary was already adorned with purple, the color of repentance and reflection. And then came the phone calls, the emergency session meetings, the rush to understand what was happening and how we should respond.

As the virus spread and the Centers for Disease Control issued increasingly urgent warnings, our church session met with a clear and solemn task: to discern how to respond faithfully to a rapidly escalating crisis. We consulted local health officials, followed the science, and prayed fervently. It quickly became clear that continuing in-person worship, with handshakes, hugs, and shared hymnals, was no longer safe. On March 15, 2020, we held our final in-person worship service for what would become an entire year.

That decision was not made lightly. For a church whose very identity is rooted in gathering, in coming together to hear God's word read and proclaimed and gather around the communion table, to close our doors felt like cutting off a lifeline. Yet we knew it was the right thing to do. We acted not out of fear but out of love for the most vulnerable among us: the elderly, the immunocompromised, the essential workers exposed daily to risk. Our guiding principle became Paul's exhortation in Phil 2:4: "Let each of you look not to your own interests, but to the interests of others."

In a letter to the congregation dated March 16, 2020, I wrote, "This is not a decision we take lightly ... but it is our belief that this is the most faithful decision we can make to live out our call to love our neighbor as ourselves." The message acknowledged the grief and disruption we all felt but reaffirmed our commitment to health, safety, and compassion. The session's unanimous vote to suspend in-person worship was not just an administrative action—it was a pastoral act of protection.

Almost immediately, we pivoted to our broadcast ministry on radio, TV, and livestreaming. Fortunately that was an easy transition for us. We have been doing radio broadcast ministry for over fifty years. We added television broadcast ministry in the 1990s. In 2018, we started livestreaming our worship services. We were grateful for the commitment the congregation had made to this form of ministry.

In those early weeks of the pandemic, we made the decision to keep worship as familiar as possible, with all of the other changes people were experiencing. So we brought in a skeleton crew of tech volunteers, our organist, and our two pastors. We livestreamed and recorded the service as if the pews were full, so that people at home could feel connected. Members of the congregation learned how to use Facebook Live and Zoom for the first time. We emailed bulletins and mailed devotionals. We improvised, stumbled, adapted, and grew.

Our associate pastor, Damen, decided that we would start recording a weekly podcast entitled "Monday Check-In." It started with me and Damen calling each other on Zoom and recording our conversation. We did a brief Bible study over the Scripture that would be preached the following Sunday followed by church announcements. This was sent out by email and posted on social media in attempt to keep people connected with the church and one another.

And through those first few chaotic months of the pandemic, something surprising happened: we remained the church. Not in the way we had always known but in ways that were deeply faithful. People tuned in to worship from their kitchen tables and living rooms. They shared comments of encouragement in the Facebook chat, lifted each other in prayer over email, and reached out to check on neighbors. The church kitchen, usually bustling on Wednesday nights, became the hub for preparing meals for delivery to isolated members. The deacons and mission committee teamed up to create a weekly phone tree to call every family in the church. Though scattered, we were not separated.

Still, the emotional toll of the pandemic was heavy. People were afraid. Many were lonely. Some were angry. And as the pandemic wore on, the divisions in our society began to seep into the life of the church.

When it came time to discuss reopening, our session approached the question with the same prayerful deliberation that had guided our initial closure. We formed a reopening task force made up of health professionals, educators, church staff, and elders. We studied public health data, read theological reflections on communal care, and held long conversations about risk and responsibility.

We sent periodic updates to the congregation. In June of 2020, I wrote, "There is no perfect solution. This is an imperfect response in an imperfect world ... What we do have is a perfect Savior who calls us to care for one another, especially the most vulnerable." Letters like these reminded our members that even difficult decisions were being made in love and faith.

The conversations were not easy. Some members urged a swift return to in-person worship, citing mental health concerns and the need for spiritual connection. Others feared for their safety and worried that reopening too soon would put lives at risk. The session listened to all voices, prayed together, and ultimately decided to err on the side of caution. We remained online for a full year, returning to in-person worship on March 14, 2021, exactly one year after our final pre-pandemic service.

Even then, our return came with clear protocols: limited seating, masked worshipers, and no congregational singing. When cases dropped during the summer of 2021, we loosened restrictions and celebrated the opportunity to worship together more fully. But when cases surged again that fall, we reinstated our mask policy and adjusted our practices. Each decision was informed by local data and guided by faith.

This decision was not universally embraced. Some members disagreed strongly, arguing that masking was unnecessary or a violation of personal freedom. A few left the church. Each departure was painful. Some were longtime members who had once served as elders, sung in the choir, or led Sunday school classes. Their absence was deeply felt.

But through the losses and disagreements, we held fast to a central conviction: our call as Christians is to care for the most vulnerable, even when it costs us something. In Rom 14:19, Paul writes, "Let us then pursue what makes for peace and for mutual upbuilding." That verse became a kind of touchstone for us, a reminder that love sometimes means choosing caution, humility, and self-restraint for the sake of others.

Our staff faced challenges too. The burden of adapting every program for online delivery, of managing technology, of fielding criticism, of navigating health guidelines—it was immense. We leaned on each other. We prayed. We cried. And, at times, we struggled.

These two years of COVID-19 disruptions taught me a great deal about the importance of listening, even when consensus is elusive. About holding space for grief and disappointment, even as we move forward. And about the quiet grace of choosing gratitude over resentment. I learned that faithfulness doesn't always mean keeping everyone happy; it means guiding with integrity, compassion, and prayer.

Throughout the pandemic, we preached and practiced the biblical vision of mutual forbearance. In Col 3:12–14, Paul writes, "As God's chosen ones, holy and beloved, clothe yourselves with compassion, kindness, humility, meekness, and patience. Bear with one another and, if anyone has a complaint against another, forgive each other. ... Above all, clothe yourselves with love, which binds everything together in perfect harmony." That was our aspiration. We didn't always live up to it perfectly, but we kept trying.

We also learned to embrace innovation. Worship services became multimedia productions. Our Advent and Lenten devotionals were delivered online and through home packets. Bible studies met via Zoom.

Session meetings became hybrid gatherings, with elders tuning in from living rooms and kitchen tables. A silver lining of the pandemic was that we became more accessible to homebound members, to snowbirds in Arizona, and to young adults living out of state. Our digital presence opened new doors.

We also came to cherish the simplicity of connection. Drive-by greetings, outdoor communion services, Zoom coffee hours: these small gestures reminded us that church is not about a building. It is about belonging. And belonging doesn't require perfection; it requires presence.

Perhaps the greatest gift of that season was clarity. We rediscovered our core values: love of neighbor, hospitality, humility, creativity, and resilience. We remembered that the church exists not just to gather but to serve. Not just to worship but to witness. Not just to endure but to adapt, grow, and thrive.

One Sunday, as we resumed in-person worship, a young family came forward to have their baby baptized. The moment felt almost surreal. Here we were, masked and distanced yet gathered again. As I poured the baptismal water into the font, I looked out over the sanctuary and saw tears in the eyes of several members as I wiped tears from my own eyes. This act, this sacrament of new life and belonging, was a sign that the church was still alive, still growing, still claiming its identity as the body of Christ.

In my final letter to the congregation in March 2022, I wrote, "For the last two years, session has faithfully prayed and discerned each time we have met. It has not been easy ... But we sacrificed our own comfort and wore masks to support the health and safety of others in our church family and our community. That stems from our faith in Jesus Christ who calls us to love one another with a self-sacrificial love."

COVID-19 did not defeat our church. It tested us. It refined us. And in many ways, it strengthened us.

As we emerged from the hardest days of the pandemic, I found myself reflecting often on Ps 46: "God is our refuge and strength, a very present help in trouble... Be still, and know that I am God."

We had been through the storm. And we were still here. Still worshiping. Still serving. Still hoping. Still finding common ground. Even when the voices clashed, even when we weren't sure what would come next, we trusted that God was in our midst. And we walked forward: masked, distanced, a little weary, but together.

Discussion Questions:

1. The church made the decision to suspend in-person worship for a full year and require masking for another year after reopening. How does this reflect the tension between personal freedom and communal responsibility? What biblical principles informed this decision?
2. The chapter explores the concept of "mutual forbearance." What does this look like in practical terms within a faith community? How can we practice it when we strongly disagree with others?
3. How can churches and other organizations manage competing expectations during conflict or crisis with grace and integrity?
4. How did your own church or community adapt during the COVID-19 pandemic? What lessons did you learn about innovation, resilience, and community?
5. Reflect on a moment during the pandemic when you experienced God's presence in an unexpected way. What did that teach you about faith and the church?

Reflection on Ps 46:1–3, 10 and Chapter 16

When the pandemic first swept into our lives in March 2020, it felt as though the earth itself had shifted beneath our feet. The familiar rhythms of worship, work, and school dissolved almost overnight. Like the psalmist, we found ourselves in a world that seemed to be trembling, where the "waters roared and foamed" in ways we had never experienced.

And yet, in that season of upheaval, the truth of Ps 46 became our anchor: God is our refuge and strength. Not the absence of trouble, not the illusion of control but God's abiding presence in the midst of it all. We discovered that refuge is not always a sanctuary filled with people but sometimes a livestream viewed from a kitchen table, a phone call from a deacon, or a meal left on the doorstep of someone in quarantine. Strength is not always about certainty but about choosing compassion when consensus is elusive, choosing patience when frustrations run high, and choosing humility when sacrifice is required for the sake of others.

The psalm also calls us to "be still and know that I am God." That stillness was not easy in a time of constant headlines, daily case counts, and endless debates. But slowly we learned that stillness does not mean passivity—it means trust. It is the quiet center where faith takes root, even when everything around us feels unstable.

Our congregation's pandemic story echoes the psalmist's conviction: the earth may change, but God does not. Even when we closed our doors, the church was not closed. Even when we were scattered, we were not abandoned. And even when we could not control the storm, we found refuge in the God who sits at the center of it all.

The promise of Ps 46 is not that the mountains will never shake but that we will not be overcome because God is in our midst. That truth carried us through the pandemic, and it carries us still.

Chapter 17

George Floyd's Impact on Small-Town Nebraska

Thus says the Lord: Act with justice and righteousness, and deliver from the hand of the oppressor anyone who has been robbed. And do no wrong or violence to the alien, the orphan, and the widow, nor shed innocent blood in this place.

Jer 22:3 (NRSV)

On the evening of May 25, 2020, George Floyd was murdered by a police officer in Minneapolis, Minnesota. The nine minutes and twenty-nine seconds that Derek Chauvin knelt on Floyd's neck were captured on video and transmitted across the country in real time, sending shockwaves through cities, suburbs, and small towns alike. We watched from Hastings, Nebraska, 530 miles away, with a mix of heartbreak, anger, and helplessness. What could we possibly do from here?

As protests and vigils began to erupt in cities across the nation, I found myself pacing around the sanctuary of First Presbyterian Church, praying the psalms of lament and asking God to show us how to respond. I didn't have to wait long.

Just six days later, on Sunday, May 31, I received a phone call from a local Lutheran pastor, Micah. His church is affiliated with the Lutheran

Church Missouri Synod, which is significantly more theologically and socially conservative than either my denomination or my congregation. Micah and I didn't know each other well at that point. He had moved to town a few months earlier and made an effort to get to know other local pastors, so we had met and chatted a bit and developed a mutual respect rooted in shared pastoral commitments.

"Greg," he said, "I've been thinking a lot about everything going on. I don't want the church in Hastings to be silent. Do you think we could do something together?"

Within twenty-four hours, Micah and I had drafted a statement:

> *Jer 22:3 (CEB)*
>
> The Lord proclaims: Do what is just and right; rescue the oppressed from the power of the oppressor. Don't exploit or mistreat the stranger, the orphan, and the widow. Don't spill the blood of the innocent in this place.
>
> The church is called to protect and care for the hurting and oppressed, and to speak out publicly against injustice. In the wake of the news of the wrongful death and murder of persons of color in our nation, we as clergy are compelled to speak publicly. We speak that all may know that God has spoken clearly and definitively, even if the church at times has been late or reluctant to do so.
>
> As pastors, we don't assume to know everything about the complexities of racism or the difficulties of law enforcement, nor have we perfected the biblical work of justice and peace-making. None of us are people of color who have faced racism directly on a daily basis. We are not police officers who are trying to do their jobs and keep the peace. We are pastors and we do the best we can to follow Jesus, to emulate his life and ministry, and to call and lead others to do likewise. This is what we know about Jesus: he came into the world because every human life has immeasurable value, for God so loved the world that he sent his only begotten son. Following Jesus means that we recognize the value in all human life, and it means that we are called to the hard work of dismantling systems that demean the value of human life.
>
> Racism is a sin. Oppression is a sin. Violence is a sin. These sins devalue human life.
>
> We believe that racism is the opposite of what God intends for humanity. It is the rejection of the other, which is contrary to the Word of God incarnate in Jesus Christ. We believe that racism is

a lie about our fellow human beings, for it says that some are less than others.

The sins of racism, oppression, and violence have impacted all of us as individuals, and they have infected the systems and structures in which we live. We have been complicit in this sin for we are a people of unclean lips who live amongst a people of unclean lips (Isa 6). The sins of racism, oppression, and violence that are in our hearts and our institutions have led to the death of innocent people, precious children of God.

As pastors, we stand united in calling out these sins we see in ourselves and our society, and we call all followers of Jesus Christ to do the same. As Christians, we are called to actively resist the sins of oppression, racism, and violence in our own lives and hearts and to actively work against these sins that are present in our systems, structures, and institutions, in the world around us, in our homes, in our workplaces, in our neighborhoods, and in the church. We are also called to authentically listen to those who are suffering and to provide an opportunity for their stories to be heard.

We also recognize the challenges that our law enforcement officers are facing. They are called to "serve and protect," and they strive to keep the peace and promote justice. Service, peace, and justice are all profoundly biblical values, and many good law enforcement officers work hard to uphold these values. We stand in support of those officers, pray for them, and encourage all Christians to do so as well.

At the same time, with the prophets of old, we publicly decry officials who abuse their authority. We call for justice to be swift, authentic, and exhaustive for law enforcement officers who fail to protect and serve members of the public. The police are given one of the highest levels of trust in our society; those who violate that trust must be placed under the full burden of the law that they wantonly disdained.

We also recognize the sin that is present in the opportunistic looting, vandalism, and violence that is occurring in cities around our country, and we speak with one voice against that sin as well.

We are a nation that is wracked with grief, anger, and profound sorrow, particularly at the untimely death of innocent people. But as Christians, we do not mourn without hope; we are resurrection people. We are called to take our resurrection hope and turn it into prayers which lead us to action.

May our prayers, in the midst of the hurt, fear, and uncertainty, be for healing of our hearts, our communities, and our

> nation. Let us fix our eyes and our prayers upon Jesus, the author and perfector of our faith. Through our prayers and our authentic engagement with our neighbors, we hope that all may come to know the sacredness of their own lives and the lives of their neighbors, particularly those neighbors who experience racism, oppression, and violence. May each of us strive to become the answer to prayers by listening deeply to the experiences of those who have suffered, embodying love, standing with our neighbors, and demanding that justice roll like a river and righteousness like a never-failing stream!

We were intentional in our language: rooting it in Scripture, centering it in our pastoral identity, acknowledging both the sin of racism and the complexity of policing. We intentionally started the statement quoting from Jer 22:3, where the prophet speaks for God, saying, "Do what is just and right; rescue the oppressed from the power of the oppressor." We confessed that racism, violence, and oppression are sins that infect not only individual hearts but entire systems. We also acknowledged that most of us clergy were white and that we hadn't personally experienced racial injustice but that we could not remain silent in the face of it.

The full statement was bold, if measured. It named hard truths but avoided slogans that might alienate the broad range of congregations we hoped would sign on. It affirmed the dignity and sacred worth of every human being. It upheld the calling of good law enforcement officers while holding space for prophetic denunciation of those who abused their power. We condemned the opportunistic violence and looting erupting in some cities—not to create a false equivalence with police brutality but to name that all forms of violence devalue human life.

Our hope was to create a middle ground where clergy across the theological and denominational spectrum could stand together. We emailed it to every pastor we knew in Hastings and the surrounding communities.

To our surprise, more than a dozen clergy signed on: Presbyterian, Lutheran, Methodist, UCC, evangelical, even a chaplain and a parachurch pastor. These weren't just progressive or moderate voices. Some were conservative, even very conservative. Some led congregations where you wouldn't necessarily expect to hear the words "racism is a sin" read from the pulpit. And yet, they signed. That was no small thing. But not everyone was satisfied.

I received a call from a fellow mainline pastor. They appreciated the intention but criticized the statement for not going far enough. "Where's the explicit call to defund the police?" they asked. "Why not name white supremacy directly?" Others felt the mention of looting undercut the central message of justice. In their view, our attempt at consensus diluted the prophetic edge, and they declined to sign on to the statement.

I understood their frustration. In some ways, I shared it. But I also believed then, and still do, that in a town like Hastings, the statement we crafted was the boldest faithful witness we could make together. It was more powerful because it reflected a collective conscience rather than a partisan position. In that sense, it was a microcosm of the kind of common ground I had been trying to cultivate in our church and our community.

The statement gained momentum when we were invited to read it publicly at a rally that took place in Hastings on June 1. According to the *Hastings Tribune*, more than three hundred people gathered on the lawn of the Adams County Courthouse. There were handmade signs, chants of "No justice, no peace," and speeches from local organizers. What struck me most was the diversity of the crowd. There were young people, many from Hastings College and our local high schools, standing alongside older residents. Several of our church youth were there, some holding signs they had made the night before in their bedrooms.

I stood beside Micah and other pastors on the courthouse steps as we took turns reading the statement aloud. It was a powerful moment: pastors from different traditions, united in our call for justice and mercy, declaring together that racism is a sin and that the church must not be silent. That moment created new possibilities.

One of those possibilities came to life just a few days later when our seminarian, an M.Div. student named Sara, reached out with an idea. "Would it be possible," she asked, "to start a conversation group about antiracism this summer? Something grounded in personal narrative, not just politics or theology, where people can tell their stories?"

We said yes. And so began a ten-week summer Zoom series titled "Stories That Transform: A Conversation about Race and Grace." It was open to anyone in the congregation, or the community, who wanted to engage in honest reflection about race, privilege, and faith. We watched the movie *Just Mercy* and read books grounded in personal narrative including *The Hate You Give*. Each week, we encouraged people to reflect and share personal stories related to race: a childhood experience, an encounter with bias, a moment of awakening. These weren't lectures or debates. They were sacred spaces.

I remember one session in particular. A woman in our church who had grown up in the South shared about learning, as a child, why her black classmates couldn't swim at the same public pool. She said she had never really talked about it before, not even with her own children. Her voice shook as she spoke. The group was silent, reverent, as she bore witness to the pain of realization and the slow work of unlearning.

Another week, a retired teacher described what it was like to see the school-to-prison pipeline play out over decades: how children of color were disproportionately disciplined, suspended, or tracked into special education. He admitted that he hadn't always known what to do but now felt a deep responsibility to be part of the solution.

Some people were tentative at first. Others spoke freely. All of them showed courage. And in those conversations, through confession, listening, grace, and truth-telling, we saw the gospel take flesh.

We didn't solve racism that summer. We didn't dismantle systems. But something changed in our church. People became more aware, more thoughtful, more open. A few started reading books and articles they had once dismissed. One church member joined a statewide anti-racism training hosted by our presbytery. Another helped launch a conversation series at her workplace. These weren't dramatic acts. But they were faithful, incremental steps toward justice.

Looking back, I see that summer as deeply meaningful. Not because we were leading marches or writing viral posts, but because we were trying, truly trying, to follow Jesus into the hard places. The Jesus who flipped tables in the temple and wept at the tomb. The Jesus who crossed boundaries to talk with Samaritans and touched the skin of lepers. The Jesus who told the truth even when it cost him.

That's the Jesus we were following in those moments: in the ecumenical collaboration with Pastor Micah, in the joint statement we penned, in the rally where we stood together, and in the sacred space of Zoom calls that created room for transformation.

But not everyone could see it that way. As the summer wore on, the fractures in the larger community, and even in the clergy community, became more visible. The pastors who didn't sign the statement, whether because it went too far or not far enough, made their positions known. One colleague criticized us for playing it too safe. Others refused to respond altogether. A few more conservative pastors privately told me they agreed with what we wrote but were afraid to alienate members of their congregations by signing on.

I don't judge them. I understand the pressures. I've felt them too. Hastings isn't Minneapolis or Portland or even Omaha. The political and social realities here require a different kind of witness: one that doesn't abandon conviction but practices it with care and humility.

If I've learned anything over the last several years pastoring a "purple church" in a deeply red state, it's this: sometimes, the most faithful witness is the one that can hold tension without collapsing into partisanship or platitudes. The gospel is political, yes, but not in the ways we often assume. It calls us to name injustice, yes, but also to build relationships that make repentance and repair possible. That's the path we tried to walk in the summer of 2020. We didn't do it perfectly. But we did it together.

And that, to me, is the heart of the story: the togetherness. A Lutheran pastor and a Presbyterian pastor, clergy from diverse traditions, youth standing with their elders, church members telling hard stories, and congregations leaning into conversations they could have easily avoided.

George Floyd's death should never have happened. But his life, and the righteous anger that followed his murder, sparked something even in small-town Nebraska. It reminded us of our common humanity. It challenged the church to speak. And it gave us a glimpse, however fleeting, of what it means to be the body of Christ in a broken world.

We still have a long way to go. Racism is still with us. Injustice still endures. But I believe that when we show up together, humbly, and honestly, we participate in the slow but sacred work of healing. May we keep showing up.

Discussion Questions:

1. In what ways did the collaborative statement from Hastings clergy balance prophetic truth-telling with pastoral sensitivity? What were its strengths and limitations?
2. How can churches in predominantly white or politically conservative areas faithfully engage in conversations about racism without becoming polarized?
3. What role does storytelling play in helping congregations confront systemic sin such as racism?

4. How do you personally respond when efforts at compromise or collaboration are criticized for "not going far enough" or for being "too political"?
5. What does it mean for the church to "show up together" in the face of injustice, and how might your own congregation embody that in your local context?

Reflection on Jer 22:3 and Chapter 17

When Jeremiah spoke these words, he was addressing a people who had grown comfortable in their religious practices but complacent in their public life. They came to the temple, offered sacrifices, and professed faith in God but failed to live out that faith in justice, mercy, and care for the most vulnerable. God's call through the prophet was clear: worship divorced from justice is empty. True devotion to God requires rescuing the oppressed and protecting the innocent.

In the summer of 2020, after George Floyd's death, those words from Jeremiah took on renewed urgency. The whole nation was confronted with the reality of injustice: the misuse of power, the oppression of Black lives, the shedding of innocent blood. Even in Hastings, far removed from Minneapolis, we could not look away. The prophet's call echoed across the centuries: "Do what is just and right."

Our clergy statement that summer tried to embody that call. We did not claim to have all the answers, but we knew silence was not an option. Like Jeremiah, we sought to name sin plainly: racism, oppression, and violence devalue human life and are contrary to God's will. We also sought to create space for humility, for confession of our own complicity, and for listening to voices too long ignored. Justice requires truth-telling, but it also requires relationships that make transformation possible.

The conversations that followed, including the rally on the courthouse lawn, the "Stories That Transform" Zoom series, and the testimonies of church members wrestling honestly with race, were imperfect but faithful attempts to live into Jeremiah's mandate. They were glimpses of what it means for the church not just to worship in stained-glass sanctuaries but to bear witness in the public square.

Jeremiah reminds us that faith without justice is hollow. And yet, when we step into the hard work of justice, however haltingly, we encounter the God who redeems and restores. To "do what is just and right" is not about political slogans or partisan allegiances. It is about embodying the heart of God, who hears the cries of the oppressed and calls the church to stand alongside them.

That summer, in a small Nebraska town, the words of the prophet came alive again. And they continue to call us forward: to keep showing up, to keep listening, and to keep choosing justice over silence, mercy over apathy, and love over fear.

Chapter 18

Powered by the "Son"

Solar Panels and Stewardship

I consider that the sufferings of this present time are not worth comparing with the glory about to be revealed to us. For the creation waits with eager longing for the revealing of the children of God; for the creation was subjected to futility, not of its own will but by the will of the one who subjected it, in hope that the creation itself will be set free from its bondage to decay and will obtain the freedom of the glory of the children of God. We know that the whole creation has been groaning in labor pains until now; and not only the creation, but we ourselves, who have the first fruits of the Spirit, groan inwardly while we wait for adoption, the redemption of our bodies. For in hope we were saved. Now hope that is seen is not hope. For who hopes for what is seen? But if we hope for what we do not see, we wait for it with patience.

—*Rom 8:18–25 (NRSV)*

In 2023, our church celebrated its 150th anniversary. One hundred and fifty years of gathering, worshiping, baptizing, burying, singing, praying, serving, and living life together in Hastings, Nebraska. For a century and a half, this congregation had weathered storms, literal and figurative, and continued to shine as a witness of God's presence in this community.

As part of the celebration, our leadership discerned that it was time to look not only backward in gratitude but also forward in hope. We launched a capital campaign, a chance to renovate our aging buildings and reimagine how we might serve future generations. Projects included updating our historic sanctuary to make our choir loft accessible, adding and updating bathrooms and public spaces, remodeling the kitchen, and upgrading accessibility across our campus. And then someone suggested something bold, something that would spark both excitement and controversy: installing solar panels on the roof of our main church building and on the roof of our community center across the street. The idea was simple enough: generate renewable energy, reduce our dependence on the local coal-fired power plant, and lower our utility bills. But nothing in Nebraska is ever that simple.

Hastings, like many communities in Nebraska, depends on coal. Our electricity comes almost entirely from a coal-fired power plant on the edge of town. When you flip on the lights in Hastings, you are burning coal. For decades, this reality has been a point of pride. Coal was reliable, plentiful, and affordable. Many in our community saw renewable energy, especially solar, as a political statement often tied to environmental activism or "coastal liberal" agendas. Suggesting solar panels in Hastings was like walking into a feed store wearing a Sierra Club T-shirt. You were bound to get looks.

We knew this would be a challenge. Some of our conservative members bristled when the idea was first floated. "Why would we waste money on something that will not work here, or will just get destroyed by hail or wind?" one member asked. Another muttered, "Solar's just a fad." Still others worried that by embracing solar, the church would appear partisan, aligning itself with one side of the political spectrum in an already polarized state. And yet, as a congregation, we chose to move forward anyway.

For me, the argument was not primarily political or even economic. It was theological. The apostle Paul, in Rom 8:18–25, writes of creation itself "groaning in labor pains," longing to be "set free from its bondage to decay." Paul's vision is cosmic. He sees all of creation swept up into God's plan of redemption. Human sin does not only affect our souls or our relationships; it distorts and damages the created world. And just as Christ redeems humanity, so too God promises to redeem creation.

If that is true, then Christians are called to participate in that work. We are not passive bystanders waiting for God to fix what we have broken. We are stewards, invited into the holy labor of restoration. That means planting trees, protecting water, conserving soil, and yes, finding ways to produce energy that does not further pollute God's good earth.

When I pitched the solar project as part of the capital campaign, I said:

"Friends, when we install solar panels on our roof, it is not only an act of prudence, it is an act of faith. It is a declaration that God's creation matters, that the earth is not disposable, and that we want our children and grandchildren to inherit a world where the skies are clear and the air is breathable. The panels on our roof are not just technology, they are testimony."

Some members resonated deeply with this message. Others did not. For some, environmental stewardship as a theological value was too abstract or too closely tied to political talking points. But there was another angle. Solar power saves money. Nebraska has abundant sunshine, and once the upfront costs are covered, solar panels provide free energy for decades. Every dollar we did not spend on electricity was a dollar we could use for ministry.

So we pitched it this way: yes, the solar project is about caring for God's creation, but it is also about stewardship of resources. The church budget is like a household budget. When the utility bill is lower, you have more flexibility for other priorities.

That message began to resonate. Members who were skeptical of the "green" language perked up when they heard about long-term cost savings. Some even suggested that the savings could be reinvested into the community. Eventually, we agreed that a portion of the savings from our lower utility bills would go into a special fund to help families in Hastings who were struggling to pay their own energy bills. Suddenly, the project was not just about solar panels, it was about serving neighbors. The environmentalists and the fiscal conservatives found themselves standing on common ground.

Every successful initiative needs champions. For us, they were Neal and Dan. Neal was a lifelong Nebraskan who had installed solar panels on his family's cabin. He loved the self-reliance and independence of generating his own electricity. He was not particularly motivated by eco-theology or carbon reduction, but he loved the freedom of watching his electric meter spin backward. Neal became a vocal advocate, reassuring skeptical members that solar really worked.

Dan, by contrast, was a theologian. A retired religion professor from Hastings College, Dan had studied and written about eco-theology for years, reading and writing works that connected Christian faith to environmental ethics. For Dan, this was not just a cost-saving measure but a spiritual discipline. He spoke of solar panels as symbols of our commitment to God's creation.

Together, Neal and Dan formed an unlikely but powerful duo—one pragmatic, the other prophetic. Neal could talk numbers and kilowatts; Dan could quote Scripture and theologians. Their partnership modeled exactly what our purple church seeks to embody: different perspectives united in common mission.

When the capital campaign officially launched, we included the solar project alongside more traditional proposals like new bathrooms and updated classrooms. We knew it might be a tough sell, but to our surprise, the congregation rallied.

In presentations about the capital campaign, we framed it clearly:

- Environmental stewardship: Do our part to reduce coal emissions.
- Financial stewardship: Save money on utilities and reinvest in mission.
- Community service: Use our savings to help neighbors with utility bills.

We emphasized that this was not an either/or but a both/and. You did not have to be a liberal environmentalist to support solar, nor a fiscal hawk to want cost savings. You could care about creation, care about budgets, or care about helping neighbors and still land in the same place.

Pledges came in. Some gave because they believed in the theology. Others gave because they liked the math. Still others gave because they trusted the leadership and wanted the church to thrive. In the end, we not only met our campaign goal—we exceeded it.

A year later, trucks pulled up and workers began installing panels on our sanctuary roof and on the community center. It was a surreal sight, cranes lifting solar panels high above stained glass windows. Tradition and innovation side-by-side.

When the system went live, we celebrated with a liturgy of dedication. We prayed over the panels, asking God to bless the sun's energy and use it for the flourishing of life. I quoted Ps 19: "The heavens are telling the glory of God, and the firmament proclaims his handiwork." And I reminded the congregation that our roof had become a visible proclamation of hope.

The results were immediate. Our electric bills dropped. In fact, today, half of the power used by our church building comes from solar, and the community center is powered entirely by the sun. Over the course of a year, we save thousands of dollars. Just as importantly, we reduce our reliance on coal, making a small but significant dent in our congregation's carbon footprint. And true to our word, we created a fund to help neighbors pay their energy bills. A mother with three kids who could not afford her utility payment received help from our "solar savings fund." An elderly man living on Social Security was able to keep his lights on thanks to our congregation's decision to harness the sun.

The solar project taught us several lessons about finding common ground in a polarized age:

- Frame the issue broadly: By presenting solar as both environmental stewardship and financial prudence, we created space for diverse motivations.
- Empower unlikely champions: Neal and Dan were very different, yet their shared advocacy built momentum.
- Connect theology to practice: Rom 8 reminded us that creation longs for redemption. Solar panels became a tangible response to that theological truth.
- Link internal savings to external service: By helping neighbors with utility bills, we ensured that the project was not just about us.
- Celebrate the witness: The panels on our roof became a public testimony. Neighbors noticed. Community members asked questions. Our church's reputation grew as a place willing to innovate and care for creation.

In many ways, this chapter of our church's story encapsulates what it means to be a purple church in a red state. We did not deny our differences. Some members still do not use the word "climate change." Others still roll their eyes at the phrase "creation care." But when the sun rises over Hastings each morning, its rays strike our panels, and our congregation collectively reaps the benefits. We found common ground in the most unlikely place, on a rooftop.

As I reflect, I am reminded again of Paul's words in Rom 8: "For in hope we were saved." Hope is not naive optimism. Hope is a gritty, determined act of faith. Installing solar panels in our community was an act of hope: hope that Christians can lead by example, hope that conservatives and liberals can collaborate, hope that creation itself can be renewed.

When I look at those panels, I see more than silicon and sunlight. I see a church choosing faith over fear, stewardship over apathy, and common ground over division. And I hear creation's groaning turn, ever so slightly, into a song of praise.

Discussion Questions:

1. How does Rom 8:18–25 shape the way Christians understand their responsibility to care for creation?
2. What does the solar panel project reveal about the possibility of finding common ground between environmental and economic concerns?
3. How do unlikely champions like Neal and Dan demonstrate the value of diverse perspectives working toward a shared goal?
4. What difference does it make that a portion of the church's solar savings is dedicated to helping neighbors pay utility bills?
5. In your own context, where might a congregation or community take bold steps that witness to hope, stewardship, and collaboration across divides?

Reflection on Rom 8:18–25 and Chapter 18

Paul paints a sweeping vision of redemption, one that extends far beyond human souls to embrace the whole of creation. He speaks of the earth itself groaning like a mother in labor, yearning for renewal. The implication is clear: the story of salvation is not just about us. It is about rivers and fields, air and soil, skies and seas. God's redemption stretches as wide as the cosmos.

When our congregation decided to install solar panels, we did so with both controversy and conviction. In Hastings, where coal power has long been a source of pride and identity, turning our faces toward the sun was not a neutral decision. For some, it looked political. For others, it looked impractical. Yet for us, it was deeply theological.

Romans 8 reminds us that the created world suffers alongside humanity, burdened by pollution, exploitation, and neglect. But it also promises that creation shares in the hope of renewal. To put solar panels on the roof of a 150-year-old church was to declare that hope is not just an abstract doctrine but a concrete practice. Each ray of sun captured by those panels became a small sign of God's larger promise: that creation will not remain in bondage forever.

What made this project powerful was not only the theology behind it but the unity it inspired. Some members were drawn to the language of ecotheology, seeing solar as part of God's call to care for the earth. Others cared about fiscal stewardship, grateful that lower bills meant more resources for mission. Still others were moved by the commitment to use our savings to help neighbors pay their own utility bills. In this way, creation's groaning met creation's hope through the hands and hearts of God's people finding common ground.

Paul says that "in hope we were saved." Hope is not passive. It is not waiting around for God to fix everything while we shrug our shoulders at the world's decay. Hope is active. It rolls up its sleeves. It plants, it builds, it innovates, it serves. Installing solar panels was not the final answer to creation's groaning, but it was a step of faith, a proclamation that we believe God's redemption includes the skies above Nebraska and the children who will breathe its air long after we are gone.

When we look at those panels, we see more than a financial investment or a technological upgrade. We see testimony. We see a church daring to hope, daring to act, daring to join creation's song of praise.

Chapter 19

Authentic Welcome, Pride Parade, and Transformation

... For I was hungry and you gave me food, I was thirsty and you gave me something to drink, I was a stranger and you welcomed me, I was naked and you gave me clothing, I was sick and you took care of me, I was in prison and you visited me." Then the righteous will answer him, "Lord, when was it that we saw you hungry and gave you food, or thirsty and gave you something to drink? And when was it that we saw you a stranger and welcomed you, or naked and gave you clothing? And when was it that we saw you sick or in prison and visited you?" And the king will answer them, "Truly I tell you, just as you did it to one of the least of these who are members of my family, you did it to me."

—*Matt 25:35–40 (NRSV)*

In the heart of a red state, in a town better known for its county fair than for pride parades, First Presbyterian Church of Hastings has slowly, quietly, and faithfully carved out a space for grace. Ours is not a story of sweeping declarations or sudden shifts. Rather, it is a story of careful steps, hard conversations, and the courage to listen. It is a story of transformation, both personal and communal, that unfolded over time, shaped not by ideology but by relationships, the nudging of the Spirit, and the deep conviction that every person is made in the image of God.

The Presbyterian Church (USA) has undergone seismic changes over the past two decades regarding human sexuality. In 2010, the denomination approved the ordination of openly gay individuals. Four years later, it authorized ministers to officiate same-sex marriages and allowed those ceremonies to take place in Presbyterian churches. These policy shifts were groundbreaking, but they also granted individual congregations the autonomy to decide how, or whether, to embrace them. In other words, the denomination made space, but it did not mandate action.

At First Presbyterian Church of Hastings, our leadership council chose a cautious path. Rather than crafting formal policy statements, we approached this with thoughtfulness and care. Our approach was not rooted in fear or avoidance but in a desire to maintain the fragile unity of a politically and theologically diverse congregation. In the early years of my pastorate, we focused on preaching love, living hospitality, and letting actions speak louder than pronouncements. We became a church that welcomed LGBTQIA+ individuals, not with fanfare or formal votes but with pews that had room and coffee that was hot and smiles that were real.

And it mattered. Slowly, people began to show up: people who had been hurt by the church elsewhere, people who had long given up on religion, and people who just needed a space where they could worship God without hiding who they were. For them, it was not about theological clarity as much as it was about being seen and loved.

One of the turning points in our journey came when a beloved church member came out as lesbian and asked to share their story with the congregation. They did not want to make a political statement or start a debate. They simply wanted to be known. After considerable discussion, we invited them to lead an adult education forum, where they spoke honestly about their experience of gender identity, faith, and community. It was vulnerable. It was brave. And it was holy.

That forum sparked a ripple effect. A few months later, we hosted the parent of a transgender teenager, a mother from another congregation who had wrestled with her child's transition and come through it with a fierce commitment to love. "I used to think this was something that happened in other families," she told us. "Now I know it can happen in any family. And what our kids need more than anything is love. They need a church that won't turn them away."

We also heard from one of our former associate pastors, who shared about his journey as a father of a transgender child. He and his wife had become vocal advocates for trans rights, navigating the medical system, school policies, and their own theological questions. They reminded us that issues that seem abstract or controversial from a distance become deeply personal when they involve your child, your family, your church.

What emerged from these forums was not unanimity of belief but something more powerful: empathy. We did not all agree on every theological or political detail. But we listened. We learned. And we grew.

In 2023, Nebraska passed legislation that restricted gender-affirming care for minors and limited the rights of transgender individuals in public life. The debate was fierce and polarizing, even by Nebraska standards. That legislation was making its way through the Nebraska Unicameral during Holy Week. We have a tradition at First Presbyterian Church where a group of church volunteers calls every member of the church during Holy Week and invites them to share prayer requests. Those requests are then used during a prayer vigil that we hold between Good Friday and Easter Sunday.

A number of people submitted prayer requests about the anti-trans legislation, and those prayers made it onto the master list that people used during the vigil. During the weekend of the vigil, some participants wrote comments in the margins of the prayer master list. While many were benign, a few were perceived as critical or dismissive of the trans community. A member of our congregation who is trans was one of the last to come through for the prayer vigil and saw the notes. She was deeply hurt. She brought the list to my office, her voice shaking, and asked, "What are we going to do about this?"

It was one of those moments when silence was not an option. We knew we had to respond with care, not defensiveness. What emerged from that painful experience was the recognition that we needed to do more than make space. We needed to be intentional about education and engagement.

In January 2024, at the urging of several church members, we organized an adult education series focused on transgender identity, faith, and advocacy. The planning team, made up of members from across the political and theological spectrum, was deliberate in inviting a diversity of voices. Our panel included our former associate pastor and his wife, who shared the joys and challenges of raising a transgender child; a licensed mental health professional who specialized in working with LGBTQIA+ youth; a biology professor from Hastings College, who brought a thoughtful and compassionate scientific perspective; and a trans member of our own congregation, who spoke with grace, depth, and quiet courage about their faith journey.

What unfolded was not a debate. It was a dialogue. People asked questions that they had never felt safe asking. Not everyone was on board. One member of our leadership council, someone who had served faithfully for years, resigned after the adult education forum. "I'm not comfortable with the direction the church is going," he told us. "It feels like we've taken a side."

I understood their concern. And I grieved their departure. But I also believed that creating space for people to tell their stories was not about taking sides. It was about living the gospel.

The next step in our journey was both bold and simple.

In the spring of 2024, the organizers of the Hastings Pride Parade reached out and asked if First Presbyterian Church would consider hosting a water station along the parade route. It was not a call to march or carry a banner. It was a request for hospitality: cold water, warm smiles, and a safe presence.

Our mission committee brought the idea to the session. The debate was thoughtful and intense. One elder said, "Some people might be upset if we do this." Another elder replied, "Some people in our church will be upset if we don't."

That comment clarified the stakes. We were no longer merely navigating resistance from outside. We were being called to accountability from within.

In the end, the session voted to host the water station. We sent out a simple announcement: volunteers were welcome. No pressure. Just an invitation.

On the day of the parade, the sun was high and the crowds were large. Our water station became a quiet beacon of grace. Church members handed out bottles of water and smiled with genuine welcome. One young person, draped in a rainbow flag, paused in front of our table and asked, "Wait … you're from a church?"

"Yes," one of our volunteers replied. "And we're glad you're here." Sometimes ministry looks like a sermon. Sometimes it looks like a bottle of water and a smile that says, "You belong."

We have never passed a formal resolution. We have never flown a rainbow flag. But we did something more daring. We lived into our calling.

We celebrated the presence and gifts of our LGBTQIA+ and nonbinary members. We welcomed without exception and preached the gospel with open arms.

Our Reformed theology gives us language for this. We believe in the sovereignty of God, which means no ideology, institution, or prejudice gets the final word. We believe in total depravity, not to shame us but to remind us that we all need God's grace to grow.

This chapter is not a victory lap. It is not the story of a church that arrived. It is the story of a church still walking, still learning, still loving. It is about a journey that began not with a statement but with a question. Who is our neighbor? And how will we love them?

The answer is not found in headlines or hashtags. It is found in the sacred ordinary: an adult education forum, a prayer vigil, a water station. It is found in the courage to stay at the table and the humility to keep listening.

And maybe most of all, it is found in the quiet but powerful act of a small-town Nebraska church saying, with word and deed: all means all.

Discussion Questions:

1. What does "quiet inclusivity" look like in your faith community? How might you move from silence to support in ways that reflect your values and context?
2. How have personal relationships with LGBTQIA+ individuals impacted your understanding of human sexuality and faith?
3. In what ways can churches support LGBTQIA+ individuals and families beyond formal statements or policies?
4. How do we navigate disagreement within a congregation while still seeking to follow Christ's command to love one another?
5. What does it mean to be a peacemaker in today's polarized cultural climate, particularly around issues of gender and sexuality?

Reflection on Matt 25:25–40 and Chapter 19

Jesus' words in Matt 25 leave little room for ambiguity. The measure of our faith is not found in lofty creeds or flawless doctrine but in whether we see Christ in the vulnerable, the marginalized, the thirsty, and the stranger. To follow Jesus is to open our eyes to the presence of Christ in those whom society ignores or even despises.

For our congregation, this truth became tangible when questions of sexuality and gender identity moved from the abstract to the personal. It wasn't about policies debated at a denominational assembly or laws passed in the Nebraska Unicameral. It was about real people in our pews: members who came out, parents who shared the journeys of their children, and neighbors who longed for a church where they would not be erased.

At times, this journey was uncomfortable. Some worried that extending hospitality meant "taking a side." Others feared what outsiders or even insiders would think. But Matt 25 reframes the conversation. Hospitality to the vulnerable is never about politics. It is about recognizing Jesus in our neighbor. It is about refusing to turn away from the thirsty, the stranger, the hurting, and instead offering water, welcome, and presence.

When our church set up a water station at the Hastings Pride Parade, the act was simple. Cold bottles of water on a hot day. Smiles and words of blessing. And yet, it was more than logistics: it was liturgy. In that moment, our congregation embodied Matt 25. To hand a cup of water to someone who wondered if they could ever belong in a church was to hand it to Christ himself. To say "we're glad you're here" was to echo God's eternal welcome.

The journey has not been without cost. Some have left, unable to walk this road. Others have stayed, learning to stretch, to listen, to grow. But through it all, we have seen the Spirit moving. We have discovered that when we risk loving boldly, we do not dilute the gospel: we deepen it.

Jesus does not ask us, "Did you agree on every issue?" or "Did you win every argument?" He asks, "When I was thirsty, did you give me something to drink? When I was a stranger, did you welcome me?"

In those questions, our calling becomes clear. Our faith is measured not by the signs on our walls but by the love in our actions. Not by whom we exclude but by whom we embrace. And when we open our doors, our hearts, and our tables to the least of these, we find ourselves in the presence of Christ.

Chapter 20

Building the Beloved Community in an Election Cycle

I give you a new commandment, that you love one another. Just as I have loved you, you also should love one another. By this everyone will know that you are my disciples, if you have love for one another.

—John 13:34–35 (NRSV)

In the summer of 2024, as another presidential election loomed on the horizon, I began to sense the rising tension in the air. Cable news talking heads were already using the language of battle. Neighbors were tiptoeing around conversations. Social media timelines were beginning to splinter again, separating friends and families into opposing digital camps. As the pastor of a politically diverse congregation, I had experienced this before. I remembered 2020. I remembered 2016. And I knew that if our church did not proactively create a space to talk about faith and politics with intentionality, we would once again risk being shaped more by the polarization of the culture than by the gospel of Christ.

So I brought an idea to our leadership council. What if, in the months leading up to the election, we preached a sermon series called "The Intersection of Faith and Politics"? What if we addressed the elephant and the donkey in the room and called our people back to the Lamb? The council liked the general direction but felt uneasy about the word "politics." For many in our church and community, politics was a trigger word. It conjured images of shouting matches, broken relationships, and moral compromise. We agreed that we needed a new title that would convey the same content but with a different tone. After some prayerful discussion, we landed on "Building the Beloved Community in an Age of Polarization."

The phrase "beloved community" has deep roots in the Civil Rights movement and in the teachings of Dr. Martin Luther King Jr. It casts a vision not merely for tolerance but for a just, inclusive, and compassionate society rooted in love. That was the vision we wanted to hold before the congregation. Not an endorsement of one political party or ideology but a call to reflect on how our faith should shape our engagement in the public square. Not an escape from the world of politics but a reimagining of what politics could look like if love was our guiding principle.

To accompany the sermon series, we launched a church-wide study of *The After Party*, a curriculum created by David French and Curtis Chang through Redeeming Babel. The premise was simple but profound: what if Christians were known not by their political combativeness, but by their posture of humility, grace, and hope? What if we could disagree politically and still remain in relationship with one another as sisters and brothers in Christ?

We organized four discussion groups each week, using the book and videos as a framework. There was a Sunday morning class that met before worship, drawing regular attendees and longtime adult education participants. On Monday nights, a group gathered at Steeple Brewery, bringing together church members and a few curious community members over pints of craft beer and conversations that ranged from the deeply theological to the humorously honest. On Tuesdays at noon, our usual Bible study group shifted to focus on the After Party themes. And on Wednesdays at noon, we held an online Zoom group, making space for those who could not attend in person or who lived out of town but had become part of our extended digital congregation.

Each group had its own character and rhythm, but all shared a common hunger. People were eager for a way to talk about politics without losing their faith or their friendships. They longed for a community where difficult conversations could be held in love and where spiritual formation did not end at the sanctuary door but extended into the voting booth, the school board meeting, and the neighborhood cookout.

The sermon series itself was carefully constructed to walk through a spiritual journey. We began with the reminder from Jas 1 and John 13 that we are called not only to be hearers of the word but doers. The world will know we are Christians not by the stickers on our cars or the slogans we recite but by our love. That Sunday, we sang the old hymn "They'll Know We Are Christians by Our Love," not as a nostalgic throwback but as a present-day challenge.

The next week, we explored what it means to bear the image of God, drawing on Gen 1 and 2 Cor 3. If every human being is made in the image of God, then we cannot reduce others to political labels or enemies. We are called to see the divine imprint in each person, even and especially in those with whom we disagree. Bearing God's image is both a gift and a responsibility. It compels us to treat one another with dignity and to reflect God's love in how we live, speak, and vote.

In the third week, we turned to the story of Abram in Gen 15 and Paul's Letter to the Ephesians, focusing on fear and hope. So much of our political polarization is rooted in fear: fear of change, fear of loss, fear of the other. But God's word to Abram is God's word to us: "Do not be afraid." We are invited to trust not in party platforms or economic forecasts but in the enduring promise of God. Hope is not naive optimism. It is rooted in the character of a God who brings life from barrenness and light from darkness.

Later in the series, we reflected on what it means to be "set apart," using the story of the first Passover in Exod 12 and 13, alongside Peter's words to the early church in 1 Pet 2. Being set apart is not about superiority or withdrawal but about living differently. The Israelites marked their doorposts with the blood of the Lamb not to escape the world but to witness to God's redeeming power within it. The early Christians were called "living stones," being built into a spiritual house. In our own time, we are set apart not by how we vote but by how we love.

Perhaps the most challenging sermon was the one on idolatry and freedom, based on the golden calf episode in Exod 32 and Paul's warning in Gal 5. We confronted the uncomfortable truth that many of us have turned political ideologies into idols. When we place more trust in a party than in the living God, when we are more loyal to a tribe than to the teachings of Jesus, we fall into the same trap as the Israelites. But Paul reminds us that we are called to a different kind of freedom. Not freedom for self-indulgence or grievance but freedom to love our neighbors as ourselves. That is the heart of the gospel and the only path to the beloved community.

Throughout the series, we kept circling back to this central idea: the beloved community is not a fantasy. It is a calling. It is not the product of human effort alone but the fruit of a Spirit-filled people who refuse to give in to the hatred and cynicism of the age. To build the beloved community is to embody the kingdom of God in the here and now, even in the messy world of elections and public discourse.

I will admit that at times, it felt like we were preaching to the choir. The folks who came to the discussion groups were the ones who already cared about these questions. They were the bridge-builders, the faithful seekers, the peacemakers. I found myself wishing that more of our polemical members would show up. Not because I wanted to change their political views but because I longed for them to experience the joy of being in dialogue across difference. I wanted them to feel the relief that comes from laying down their armor and stepping into a space shaped by grace.

And yet, I also recognized that in a polarized age, just holding space for faithful conversation is itself an act of resistance. Every time someone chose to listen instead of lash out, every time someone said, "I never thought of it that way before," we were chipping away at the walls that divide us. These may seem like small acts, but I believe they are sacred. They are the building blocks of beloved community.

There were quiet moments of transformation. A lifelong Republican and a committed Democrat sat together at the brewery and discovered that they shared the same concerns about poverty and immigration, even if they had different policy preferences. A retired farmer asked a young teacher how schools were handling civics education, and they ended up praying for one another. An elder in the church admitted in the online group that he had never read anything by David French before but found his insights compelling. These were not headline-grabbing stories. But they were holy moments.

As a preacher, I felt the tension every week. I knew that some were listening for clues, trying to discern if I was subtly endorsing one candidate or another. I worked hard to keep the focus on Scripture, not soundbites. I tried to name sin without demonizing people. I wanted to be prophetic but also pastoral. I prayed over every sermon and discussion, asking God to give me courage and compassion in equal measure.

Looking back, I am grateful we did it. It was not perfect. We did not reach everyone. But we planted seeds. We reminded the congregation that their primary identity is not as Democrats or Republicans, not even as Americans, but as disciples of Jesus Christ. We reaffirmed that civic engagement is a form of stewardship and that voting is both a privilege and a responsibility. And we modeled a way of being together that does not require uniformity of thought but calls for unity of spirit.

If I could offer one encouragement to other pastors or congregations considering something similar, it would be this: do it. Step into the conversation. Name the polarization. Offer a different way. But do so with humility, with kindness, and with deep grounding in Scripture. Trust that the Holy Spirit will show up. Trust that love is stronger than fear. And remember that the beloved community is not built in a single sermon series or a single election cycle. It is built day by day, person by person, prayer by prayer.

As the election approached, our church was not immune to the tension. Some yard signs appeared. Some heated Facebook posts were shared. But I also saw people choosing to stay at the table. I saw members praying for our leaders, regardless of party. I saw love that refused to be shaken by disagreement. And in those moments, I caught a glimpse of the kingdom. Not a utopia, not a sanitized consensus, but a real community grounded in grace.

This is what I believe the purple church can offer in a divided world. Not answers to every policy debate but a posture of love. Not a blueprint for national unity but a living witness to the reconciling power of Christ. We are called not to escape the world of politics but to redeem it by how we live and love within it. That is the call of the beloved community. May we continue to build it, brick by brick, heart by heart.

Discussion Questions:

1. What does the term "beloved community" mean to you? How does this vision challenge or deepen your understanding of what the church can be during divisive political times?
2. Which modern idols—such as political loyalty, grievance, or fear—do you see most commonly pulling people away from community and compassion? How might Gal 5's vision of freedom through love help us resist these idols?

3. Have you ever experienced a meaningful conversation across political or ideological lines within a faith setting? What made it possible, and what can the church do to create more spaces like that?
4. The chapter names both prophetic and pastoral roles when preaching during an election cycle. What do you think are the challenges and responsibilities of faith leaders when addressing political or cultural polarization?
5. Building the beloved community is described as a long-term process, "brick by brick, heart by heart." What is one "brick" you can contribute—one action, habit, or relationship—that helps build a more loving and united community in your church or neighborhood?

Reflection on John 13:34–35 and Chapter 20

On the night before his death, Jesus could have given his disciples a hundred instructions. He could have told them how to navigate political powers, how to build religious institutions, or how to survive the hardships that were to come. Instead, he gave them one clear command: love one another. This, he said, would be the defining mark of Christian identity: not purity of doctrine, not political allegiance, not moral superiority, but love.

In the summer of 2024, as another election cycle loomed, our congregation leaned into that command with intentionality. We knew what polarization could do to families and churches because we had seen it before. We knew how quickly suspicion could creep in and how quickly arguments could drown out empathy. But Jesus' words called us back to our truest center: discipleship defined by love.

Our sermon series, "Building the Beloved Community in an Age of Polarization," and our study of *The After Party* curriculum became a living laboratory for this commandment. Week after week, people from across the political spectrum sat down together, not to agree on candidates or policies but to practice what it means to love one another as Christ has loved us.

That love took tangible form:

- A Republican and a Democrat discovered they shared a common concern for children in poverty.
- A farmer and a teacher prayed for one another.

- Members who once assumed they had nothing in common learned to listen with humility.

These were not grand, headline-making gestures. They were ordinary acts of love. Yet they carried extraordinary weight because they pushed back against the lie that politics must always divide us.

Jesus' commandment in John 13 is radical precisely because it is so simple. It insists that love—sacrificial, patient, Christ-shaped love—becomes the signpost by which the world recognizes us as his disciples. In a polarized age, that is perhaps the most countercultural act we can perform.

The commandment of Jesus has not changed. Our challenge is to live it in the particular context of our time. In Hastings, Nebraska, in the heat of an election cycle, that looked like creating spaces where love could guide political conversations, where discipleship was measured not by uniformity but by unity, and where our witness was not "we are right" but "we are loved and therefore we love."

And maybe that is the greatest gift the church can offer a divided nation: a reminder that there is another way. A way marked not by fear but by love. A way in which, by God's grace, everyone will know we are his disciples.

Chapter 21

Finding Joy in a Purple Church

Rejoice in the Lord always; again I will say, Rejoice. Let your gentleness be known to everyone. The Lord is near. Do not worry about anything, but in everything by prayer and supplication with thanksgiving let your requests be made known to God. And the peace of God, which surpasses all understanding, will guard your hearts and your minds in Christ Jesus.

—*Phil 4:4–7 (NRSV)*

On any given Sunday at First Presbyterian Church of Hastings, Nebraska, you'll find a congregation that defies easy categories. A rancher with calloused hands and conservative politics passes the peace to a retired professor who has marched in more than one protest. A young family with rainbow stickers on their minivan listens intently as an elder who served in Vietnam reads Scripture from the pulpit. After the benediction, a retired teacher invites a new immigrant family to join the line for coffee and donuts. People linger. They talk. They laugh. And when it's time to clean up, they do it together.

This is what it looks like to be a purple church in a red state.

That phrase, "purple church," has followed me throughout this journey. At first, it simply meant what it sounds like: a congregation composed of both red and blue voters, a theological and political blend in a polarized land. But over time, I've come to understand the phrase more deeply. Liturgically, purple is the color of repentance and preparation. It marks the seasons of Advent and Lent, the time before birth and the time before resurrection. Purple holds within it both anticipation and sorrow, both humility and hope. A purple church, then, is not just politically mixed; it is spiritually tuned to the tension and possibility of transformation. It is a church willing to wait, to wrestle, and to walk toward something more faithful and more joyful than either red or blue alone could ever offer.

This book has traced the journey of our purple church. It began with my own call to Hastings in 2017, a time when the nation was still reeling from the 2016 presidential election. The divisions in our country felt sharper than ever. I arrived wondering how I would preach the gospel in a place where members of the same congregation had voted for candidates who could not have been more different. What I discovered, over time, is that the gospel is big enough for that. In fact, it is precisely in such spaces of tension that grace can grow.

In those early months, I learned that the key to serving a purple church was not to ignore difference but to ground everything in love. I found hope in peanut butter and jelly sandwiches, in sack lunches packed by volunteers who might disagree on policy but could agree that no child in our community should go hungry. I saw how mission could transcend partisanship, how service could soften suspicion.

When historic flooding struck Nebraska in 2019, we didn't gather to debate the causes or argue about federal response. We rolled up our sleeves. We delivered supplies and traveled to the Pine Ridge Reservation to help neighbors rebuild. No one asked who had voted for whom. They asked, "What do you need? How can we help?" Crisis revealed our shared humanity and our deep capacity for compassion.

That same spirit of unity emerged again during the COVID-19 pandemic. The decisions we made—shutting down in-person worship, enforcing mask requirements, shifting to online services—were not easy. They provoked disagreement and disappointment. But they were made with prayer, with humility, and with a commitment to protect the vulnerable. I will never forget the resilience of our congregation in those months: deacons and the mission committee calling every church member, drive-up communion, musicians recording and editing anthems from their homes. The building may have been closed, but the church never stopped being the church.

The pandemic also prompted deeper questions: What does it mean to be the body of Christ when we are apart? What binds us together when we cannot share the same space? The answers came slowly, often in surprising ways. A Zoom Bible study where a retired farmer and a college student wrestled with the Psalms. A Sunday school class that discussed racial justice in the wake of George Floyd's murder. A socially distanced vigil. We learned that the gospel doesn't require uniformity. It requires love, courage, and commitment.

Our response to racial injustice became a defining chapter in our story. In the summer of 2020, as protests filled streets across the country, our congregation found its own voice. In partnership with other churches, we made a public statement on racism. Some found it too bold. Others thought it didn't go far enough. But it was honest. It was shared. And it became the starting point for ongoing conversations about equity, repentance, and justice.

We continued our decades-long partnership with Frontera de Cristo, building bridges across borders and cultures. Our mission trips to the US-Mexico border were not just acts of service. They were acts of listening, of learning, of mutual transformation. The songs we sang in English and Spanish, the meals we shared with migrant families, the prayers we offered beside the border wall: these were moments when the body of Christ felt wide and wondrous, and we began to see immigration issues through the eyes of and heart of our faith.

Back home, we found similar power in simple acts of care: free haircuts for schoolchildren, shared meals around tables, Sunday night suppers where people with nothing in common found common ground in casseroles and conversation. Table fellowship became a theology in motion. As the hymn says, "We are one in the Spirit, we are one in the Lord … and they'll know we are Christians by our love." That became our goal: not to be right but to be known by our love.

Even the issues that many churches avoid—gun violence, immigration, LGBTQIA+ inclusion—became opportunities for us to practice grace. We did not always agree. But we learned to listen without shouting, to speak without shaming. We hosted forums, held vigils, preached sermons, and shared stories. We opened the doors and trusted that the Spirit would guide us through.

Our journey has been slow, intentional, and rooted in relationship. We don't necessarily pass bold resolutions or issue press releases. We listen.

We learn. We try to make room. We offer food for the hungry, drink to the thirsty, and welcome to the stranger. And when someone asks, "You're from a church?" we say, "Yes. And we're glad you're here."

Being a purple church does not mean being neutral or noncommittal. It means being present. It means showing up with compassion even when it's complicated. It means loving our neighbor even when our neighbor challenges our assumptions. It means holding tension not as a problem to solve but as a sacred space where grace can unfold.

To serve a purple church is to live in that space every day. It is to preach to a congregation where some think the sermon was too political and others think it wasn't bold enough. It is to sit in session meetings where elders quote both Micah and the US Constitution. It is to love without caveat, to lead without fear, and to trust that God is at work even in our disagreements.

I have learned more about the gospel from this congregation than I could have imagined. I have seen people forgive one another, challenge one another, and walk alongside one another in ways that defy political logic. I have seen conservatives serve communion to progressives. I have seen liberals offer prayers for politicians I know they didn't vote for. I have seen children lead us into joy and elders call us back to hope.

And above all, I have seen joy.

Yes, there have been hard moments. We have lost members. We have faced criticism. We have made mistakes. But we have also laughed. We have celebrated. We have shared potlucks and bluegrass music, baptisms and birthday cakes. We have found joy not in sameness but in shared purpose.

The joy of being a purple church is the joy of watching the Spirit do something new, something no political party or theological tribe can claim. It is the joy of resurrection after division, of community after conflict. It is the joy of knowing that Christ is bigger than our boxes and more beautiful than our binaries.

As we look to the future, we do not have a five step plan for how to fix polarization in the church or in the country. But we do have a witness. We have seen what is possible when people choose love over fear, presence over withdrawal, listening over shouting. We have seen the kingdom of God come near, not in grand gestures but in small, consistent acts of kindness, courage, and faith.

If you are reading this and are part of your own purple church, or longing to build one, know this: it is possible. It is holy. And it is worth it.

Red and blue may define our divisions. But purple? Purple is the color of promise, of possibility, of preparation. Purple is the color of the in-between, the already and not yet. Purple is the color of churches who dare to believe that love really can make a way.

And when we live in that purple space, when we find common ground and stand on holy ground, we find something else too.

We find joy.

Invitation for Reflection:

As you reach the end of *Purple Church, Red State*, pause and reflect on the story you've just read and your own context:

1. Where have you witnessed the beauty and challenge of being part of a politically or theologically diverse community? It doesn't have to be a church, but what "purple" spaces are you a part of?
2. What stories, images, or moments from this book will stay with you?
3. How is God calling you to live into the vision of a beloved community in your own place?
4. What does "joy" look like in the life of your congregation?
5. How can you be a bridge-builder, a listener, and a witness to love in the season ahead?

Reflection on Phil 4:4–7 and Chapter 21

When Paul wrote these words to the Philippians, he was not living in ease or comfort. He was writing from prison, uncertain of his future, and yet his letter is full of joy. Not superficial happiness but a deep, sustaining joy rooted in Christ. Joy that transcends circumstance. Joy that holds together communities under pressure. Joy that makes gentleness possible, peace attainable, and hope durable.

That same kind of joy is what I have witnessed at First Presbyterian Church of Hastings. Ours is a congregation that does not deny its political, theological, and generational differences. We are, by all accounts, a purple church. And yet, like the Philippians, we have discovered joy in Christ that is stronger than division.

I have seen it in potlucks, where casseroles and laughter flow more freely than partisan talking points. I have seen it in sack lunch assembly lines, where people who disagree about policy stand shoulder-to-shoulder, making sure no child goes hungry. I have seen it in vigils and mission trips, where tears of lament mingle with songs of hope. I have seen it in the quiet moments after worship, when neighbors linger over coffee and remember that belonging is not about agreement but about grace.

Philippians reminds us that joy is not found in being right or in winning arguments: it is found in the nearness of the Lord. When we know Christ is near, we can loosen our grip on fear and worry. We can bring our requests to God in prayer, trusting that the peace of Christ will guard our hearts even when the world feels unstable.

To be a purple church is, in many ways, to live Phil 4 in real time. It is to rejoice always, not because everything is easy but because God is faithful. It is to let gentleness be known: not weakness but a strength clothed in compassion. It is to pray with thanksgiving in all things, knowing that every act of kindness, every shared meal, every hard conversation held in love is part of God's work of peace among us.

Over the years, I have come to see that our differences are not obstacles to joy: they are the soil in which joy grows. Joy emerges when people forgive one another, when they listen across divides, when they choose to remain in relationship even when it would be easier to walk away. Joy blooms in the purple space where red and blue blend into something new: a witness that the gospel is big enough for all of us.

This joy is not naive. It knows the pain of loss, the frustration of disagreement, the exhaustion of living in polarized times. But it also knows resurrection. It knows that Christ is risen, the Spirit is present, and God is still making all things new. That is why Paul could rejoice from a prison cell and why we can rejoice in a purple church in Nebraska.

In the end, this is our witness: that even in a divided land, there can be communities of gentleness, prayer, peace, and joy. And that when we live this way, when we dare to rejoice always, to trust God with our fears, and to embody Christ's love, the world will catch a glimpse of the kingdom of God in our midst.

Epilogue

WHEN I FIRST OUTLINED this book in the fall of 2024, I knew we were headed into another contentious election cycle. I had lived through the fractures of 2016 and 2020, and I suspected that 2024 would bring more of the same. But I could not have fully anticipated the climate we now find ourselves in, months into 2025. The rhetoric has grown sharper, the divisions deeper, and some of the policies emerging from our nation's leaders bear a cruelty that wounds the most vulnerable among us. Even more painful is seeing religion used to justify such cruelty: Scripture twisted to excuse exclusion, the name of Christ invoked not to heal but to harm.

There are moments when I question whether a "purple church" is even possible in such a time. Holding space for people of different convictions, practicing patience in the face of fear, seeking common ground when the loudest voices demand sides—it can feel like standing in a raging storm with nothing but a tiny flickering light. And yet, I have also learned that the light shines in the darkness, and the darkness does not overcome it.

The story of God's people has never been free from hardship. Prophets cried out against leaders who used faith to prop up power. Jesus himself challenged religious authorities who placed burdens on the weak while neglecting mercy and justice. Paul wrote to churches fractured by culture, class, and conflict, urging them to hold fast to love. Again and again, Scripture reminds us that cruelty does not have the final word and that God's light shines brightest when the night seems darkest.

That is where I choose to place my trust. Not in political platforms or human power but in the God who raised Jesus from the dead. Not in the noise of division but in the quiet persistence of love that shows up in sack lunches, water stations, vigils, meals shared, and neighbors welcomed. These small acts of faithfulness are not small at all; they are seeds of the kingdom, signs of resurrection, glimpses of the beloved community.

So, yes, I still have doubts. I still wonder if the work of building bridges and holding space can withstand the forces that tear at our common life. But alongside my doubts, I cling to hope. Hope that the Spirit is still at work among us. Hope that churches like ours, imperfect as we are, can be witnesses to a love greater than our divisions. Hope that even in this season, Christ's command still holds: "Love one another. By this everyone will know you are my disciples."

This book began as a reflection on what it means to be a purple church in a red state. It ends with a benediction of sorts: a blessing for all who long for a different way. May you not lose heart. May you not give in to fear. May you find joy in small acts of faithfulness. And may you keep your eyes fixed on Jesus, the one who heals, who feeds, who forgives, and who makes all things new.

And so, as we go from these pages back into the world, may we not lose heart. The divisions are real, the cruelty is real, the misuse of faith is real, but so is the love of Christ and our call as disciples to share that love with the world in word and deed. I want to close the pages of this book as I close every worship service at First Presbyterian Church of Hastings, with this charge and blessing:

Go out into the world in peace. Have courage. Hold fast to what is good. Return no one evil for evil. Strengthen the faint-hearted. Support the weak. Help the suffering. Honor and serve all people and all creation. Love and serve the Lord your God, following the example of Jesus Christ, and rejoicing in the power of the Holy Spirit and abides with you. Go in peace. Amen.

Scripture Index

www.ingramcontent.com/pod-product-compliance
Lightning Source LLC
LaVergne TN
LVHW020627100826
845148LV00012B/2085

* 9 7 9 8 3 8 5 2 5 6 8 7 7 *